Cockshut, A
    The imagination of
Charles Dickens

THE IMAGINATION OF
CHARLES DICKENS

The
Imagination of
CHARLES
DICKENS

A. O. J.
COCKSHUT

NEW YORK UNIVERSITY PRESS
1962

To Shenka

Contents

Preface

No book on Dickens can reasonably aim at completeness. The subject is too vast, and in any case some excellent work has already been done. On the whole the most distinguished critics of Dickens have made a sharp distinction between the popular idol and the artist. Thus Mr. Ford in *Dickens and his Readers* writes of what he meant to a vast international audience; the late Humphry House placed him brilliantly in his setting of legislation and social change; and Mr. Hillis Miller, Professor Trilling and other American critics have written of him mainly as a subtle and complicated classic.

I have learnt from all these, but unlike them, my aim has been to show that the popular idol and the great artist are not only the same person, but completely inseparable for criticism. His melodramatic bias, his sympathy with popular taste, were the indispensable means by which his more profound gifts became productive.

I have also tried to show a continuous development and enrichment of his mind and art from *Pickwick* to *Our Mutual Friend*. I am conscious of an important omission in *Edwin Drood*, his last, unfinished book. But fascinating as it is, it seems too enigmatic to occupy a clearly-defined position in the line of development traced here. I hope to write on *Edwin Drood* elsewhere.

Dickens's development was very complex, of course. But I have stressed in particular the development of certain simple ideas, prisons, crowds, justice, money and dirt, which seem to have been fundamental for him. It was not primarily a progress of ideas or opinions, but an ever deeper penetration into the majestic range of possible meaning contained in the simple ideas and images of his youth. For an understanding of this development, dates are important, and instead of a full bibliography which might be confusing, a simple list of the dates of works discussed at any length in the text is placed at the end.

I wish to acknowledge my debt to Edgar Johnson's excellent biography of Dickens. Like him, I have felt it necessary to say some hard things about the man and the writer. But right at the start, I put on record my conviction that Dickens was one of the few who are truly great.

A.O.J.C.

I

Introductory

In the last twenty-five years, Dickens has advanced from the "classics" shelf in the preparatory school library to the position of a real and acknowledged classic. The process by which the best-seller whom many clever people despise achieves classic status would repay attention from sociologists. But for my purpose, two questions are raised: How did a man with such a coarse mind become a master of his art? and, How was it possible, in the nineteenth century, to be a best-seller and a true classic at the same time?

The artistic handicaps inherent in his mind certainly seem at first sight formidable enough. He was not a man who could be deeply influenced by literature. It seems likely that, to the end of his days, he never came to understand himself or his own motives very well. He lacked the disinterested curiosity, and the detachment which are indispensable for profound spiritual or intellectual development. He never attained any deep understanding of history, art or politics. His general critical comments are, without exception, jejune and superficial, and show that he never progressed very far beyond his simple boyish enthusiasm for Fielding and Smollett. His prefaces reveal a literal mind, and a determination to prove that his strangest imaginative flights are only sober reporting.

An examination of the text of his works shows that some of the qualities in which he is reputed to be strong are largely fortuitous or even non-existent. Thus, Dickens, more perhaps than anyone else, is regarded as the founder of our modern version of Rousseauist innocence. When people talk about the fundamental decency of the working class, they are often influenced by Dickens. This is odd, for two reasons. First, owing to the uncomfortable pseudo-gentility of his family, and his early bitter experience of being treated in the blacking factory as a member of the working class, Dickens was very class-conscious. It is significant that all his heroes (except in *Hard Times*, which provides exceptions to several fair generalisations) speak the King's English, even when it is impossible to understand how they can have learnt it. But such is his melodramatic power, and the sympathy he excites for outcasts like Smike, who are helped and patronised by his gentlemanly heroes, that many people actually think that he wrote mainly about the working class.

But there is another and more fundamental reason for surprise that this myth of proletarian innocence finds an important source in Dickens. It is really the darkness of their surroundings, and the hypnotic power of their enemies that make his threatened innocents so influential. If you stop a man in the street and ask him to name a Dickens character, he may mention a purely comic figure, but it is just as likely that he will name a threatened innocent like Oliver Twist. But no one would have remembered Smike if it had not been for Squeers, and no one would have remembered Oliver if it had not been for Fagin. Moral goodness in Dickens exists largely by contrast. The goodness of those who are not isolated or threatened, like the Cheeryble brothers, is frequently absurd, or at the least, even in his mature vein, pale and faintly embarrassing like that of John Jarndyce and Esther.

Dickens failed here because he had absolutely no conception of sanctity. A writer has spoken recently of the "religious inanity of our greatest novelist." If the compliment is scarcely too high, the blame, too, is scarcely too severe. Dickens's religion, a kind of loose, moralistic Anglicanism-cum-unitarianism, was perfectly sincere. But as the above confused definition will indicate, it lacked consistency. Worse still, it was cut off from the spiritual and intellectual treasures of the Christian tradition. When he was really thinking, he unconsciously assumed that religion was irrelevant; and it seems likely, too, that emotional and indeed sentimental though its expression often was, it did not operate at a level where it could mingle with his deepest and most persistent feelings.

His innate melodramatic tendency, though, as I shall try to show, an advantage to him in many ways, was no help here. It left him very imperfectly aware that good and evil exist together in the same person, and therefore unaware also of the difficulty of living up to one's own standards. The Cheeryble brothers are unconvincing largely because they never seem to have known an impulse to be ungenerous. In reading Dickens, it is apt to seem rather easy to be good, or as good as Dickens expects you to be. Hence, at his worst, he tends to encourage pharasaism. He was, on the technical side, profoundly conservative; and melodramatic conventions appealed to him for their solid, traditional strength. They appealed also to his engrained love of violence. He was able to become a great artist without ever ceasing to be crudely melodramatic. (Think, for instance, in two of his best books, of the Dedlock mystery, and Boffin's salvation from the clutches of miserdom.) In this, and especially in the way he was fascinated all his life by the subject of murder, he can fairly be compared with a master who no doubt surpassed him, but who nevertheless learnt much from him—Dostoevsky. In the conservative nature of his technical originality, he can be called Shakespearian. At all times it was both his strength and weakness that he immersed himself completely in his work. A letter of 7th January 1841 to Forster about Little Nell was typical of his lifelong attitude to his creations. " It casts the most horrible shadow upon me, and it is as much as I can do to keep moving at all. I tremble to approach the place a great deal more than Kit. . . . I have refused several invitations for this week and next, determining to go nowhere till I had done." Even at his worst, Dickens cannot be dull. He hypnotised the reader because he hypnotised himself.

II

It does not seem useful to inquire here into possible biographical sources of his favourite images. It would be easy, though perhaps mistaken, to link some of them to experiences of his early years. Thus both the prison and the money obsession could be explained by the fact that his father was imprisoned for debt. But what matters for the evaluation of his novels is that he already had an obsession with these things at the start of his career in *Pickwick Papers*, and that he had it still in *Our Mutual Friend*. So it is that his work, as much as anyone's should be seen as a continuous whole. There are some irregularities in the pattern, naturally, to remind us that we are dealing with an unpredictable human being. There are moments in *David Copperfield*, for instance, when he seems to revert to an earlier style. But taken as a whole, the development is extraordinarily continuous. The stock of ideas and images hardly varies; the profundity of their meaning and the skill of their arrangement develop prodigiously. The lack of spiritual and intellectual development is excused by the wonderful development in imagination and technique.

His intense awareness of physical objects was necessary to him as a symbolist; and it was necessary in other ways too. For in constant tension with his sense of facts and objects was his bias towards fantasy. Sometimes fantasy was too strong. I give in the chapter on prisons my reasons for thinking that this is so in the case of *Pickwick Papers*. But even in this book fantasy was not completely out of control. The fantasies of Dickens, like those of Mrs. Gamp, were very earthy—and, despite some failures, the tension between fantasy and obsessive sensibility to detail was very fruitful.

One might say that his abiding and ever-increasing sense of the pressure of life, and his advancing technical skill gradually compressed and solidified the volatile essences of his early fantasy. The light and airy *Pickwick Papers* was transformed into the weighty bulk of *Our Mutual Friend* or *Great Expectations*. So his later books give the impression of having been formed under pressure like geological strata. This disciplining, and partial elimination of his sparkling fantasy was necessary for achievement of his best works; but it was not all gain. The greatest casualty in the process was his humour.

2

Humour,

Positive and Negative

The humour of Dickens is his best-loved contribution to our life; and perhaps his most influential, for most English humorous writing since his time unconsciously imitates him. So it is hard to realise how far he lies outside the various humorous traditions of earlier times. His best humorous writing is only very mildly satirical. When he became deeply satirical, his humour declined, as we shall see. Chaucer, Ben Jonson, the Augustan satirists and the eighteenth-century novelists, all required for their humorous effects an accepted moral system and the idea of a society as an organic body in which functions varied. Now Dickens ultimately showed that he, too, could work from this basis; but in his most characteristic early comic writings, his moral sense and his vision of corporate society were in abeyance.

He is faintly linked with Augustan satire by his use of mock-heroics. But very faintly, because he uses it so crudely as to make any detailed comparison with Pope absurd, and even Fielding easily surpasses him. A comparison with Shakespeare is slightly more rewarding, but even in the passages where Shakespeare's humour comes nearest to Dickensian extravagance, in the mechanicals of *A Mid-*

summer Night's Dream, there is an awareness of class and society.

Another obvious fact, likely to be obscured by our great familiarity with Dickens's humour, is that he tends to ignore the traditional comic subject. Smollett is an example of a comic writer of moderate talents only whose humour derives mainly from the fact that a few subjects are funny in themselves. Writing of adultery, fisticuffs or dung the author need contribute very little. The basic humorous brutality of the race will do most of his work for him. The relation between the sexes, in particular, normally the chief field of comic invention, is almost completely ignored by Dickens when not in a serious vein. When he does attempt to portray comic husband-hunting and nagging wives, he usually fails through mixing fantasy and seriousness in impossible proportions. We can never be quite happy about laughing at Mercy and Charity Pecksniff.

Nor does Dickens often resort to the traditional humour of situation—people going into the wrong bedroom, listeners hearing frank comments on themselves, mistaken identity and the like. The encounter of Parson Adams with Parson Trulliber in *Joseph Andrews* is a good example of this tradition of the theatre neatly acclimatised in the novel. Dickens ignores such devices.

Some of Dickens's least successful humour, it is true, harps on the subject of drink, which was just developing into a stock comic subject in his time, and has remained one ever since. This development, which only slightly concerns us here, would be worth investigating. It would seem that, in a time of mounting literary solemnity about sex, and of the rise of total abstention as a moral ideal, drink partly took the place of sex, to supply the indispensable comic mystery of forbidden fruit.

But with one or two minor reservations like these, we

can say that the humour of Dickens was truly creative and original. It is derived largely from idiosyncrasies of language, showing forth impossible eccentricity. It lacks the morality, the good sense, the analysis of the typical follies and inconsistencies of human nature, which is the main strength of comic tradition. Instead it reveals new abysses of absurdity, fantastic and yet hypnotically real to the reader, in characters who fall outside normal canons of judgment. If I risk inventing the terms positive and negative humour, to distinguish the two kinds, it is, of course without any suggestion that the positive type is superior. On these terms, Jonson's humour would be called negative, because his characters were seen to be failing to meet a standard of religion, morality and good sense, and to be absurd because of their failure. Dickens's is, usually, positive, because his great comic creations, Crummles, Mrs. Gamp, Mr. Micawber, present forms of absurdity not to be found in human nature, and therefore hardly amenable to moral categories. It is this "positive" quality that makes the humour of Dickens so difficult to analyse, and so easy to enjoy. Negative humour, in the hands of a master like Ben Jonson, makes for the greatest moral profundity and the greatest artistic unity. But positive humour is perhaps the purest, the most memorable—in fact, the *funniest* form. It can be traced back to a few passages in Shakespeare, a few speeches of the Fool in *Lear* and of Autolycus and Bottom. But after Dickens, and excepting his imitators, who are mostly inferior, we have only the Victorian nonsense writers and P. G. Wodehouse. Splendid as these are, they do not prevent Dickens from reigning supreme.

II

Particular attention should be paid to the private languages of his characters. And here a comparison with Scott may be helpful. Take the brilliant comic (and serious) passage in *Old Mortality* where the time-serving son, Cuddie saves his fanatical mother, Mause Headrigg from the Stuart soldiery by means of a verbal confusion between the covenant of works and the covenant of grace. Here is a fine, complex example of what I have called negative humour. The context is rich. The whole Reformation controversy about faith and works, Calvinism, Arminianism and Pelagianism lurk behind the passage. The humour lies partly in the ignorance of the soldiers, who cannot see the immense theological gulf between the two covenants, partly in the crafty, worldly use of theological learning by Cuddie, and partly in the sublime, naïve truthfulness of Mause, who curses the covenant of works with the deepest sincerity, unaware that she is being guided by her son into a skilful deception. Theology is here truly alive; words like "covenant" recapture the primitive terror and force felt by those who first used them. At the same time the Scottish dialect of the characters is central to the traditions of the people. It is a heightened form of a common, public language. The passage is very funny, but it is potentially tragic, too. Martyrdom is very near, and Mause would not shrink if it came.

As if to underline the colossal difference between Mause and Mrs. Gamp, there is one similarity. Mrs. Gamp also speaks in the language of religious consolation. Here are a few of her strange religious phrases, chosen almost at random:

This Pilgiams Projiss of a mortal wale.

Playing at berryin' down in the shop, and follerin' the order book to its long home in the iron safe.

Rich folk may ride on camels, but it isn't so easy for 'em to see out of a needle's eye.

Lambs would not forgive, nor worms forget.

The families I've had . . . would take a week to chrisen in Saint Polge's fontin.

The relation of the multitude of remarks of this kind to the religious rhetoric from which they derive is complicated. Mrs. Gamp is not a hypocrite, like Pecksniff; she is not making fun of the religious sentiments of others, or trying to compose a witty parody. It is rather that a tradition of religious sensibility has plunged right down into the unconscious memory of the race, and has risen once again to the surface, filtered through this strange personality, deprived of its order and logic, a recreated, original Gampian language. Part of its strange power is due to the religious tradition behind it; but the satirical element we would expect is absent. There is no criticism of religious doctrines, or of Mrs. Gamp for perverting them (as there would be in Scott). In the end, derivative though it is, the language stands on its own, and we enjoy it for its own sake. The vast context present in *Old Mortality* dwindles to nothing. Mrs. Gamp's language is detached; it is like a volcanic island. Powerful subterranean forces may have formed it, but we forget them when we see the island's own individual beauty. In the same metaphor, Scott's humour could be compared to a perfectly produced picture of all the geological strata that went to produce the final result.

This is particularly odd when we think of Mrs. Gamp's social position. As a midwife and a nurse she is the cause of terrible sufferings. With a slight change in the point of view, the story could become charged with moral indignation. Florence Nightingale, one might say, spent her life in displacing and defeating Mrs. Gamp. But all this, undeniable though it is, seems curiously irrelevant to the actual literary quality of the woman. Her voice stills all questionings and puts all general values out of account. In part, this effect is achieved by the deliberate breaking down of logical categories. For instance, she says, "A pleasant evening, though warm, which we must expect when cowcumbers is three for twopence." It is natural to Mrs. Gamp, and in reading about her, it becomes curiously natural to us, to make the weather depend on prices, instead of the other way about.

At the same time, phrases like, " Gamp is my name, and Gamp my nater," though literally meaningless, have a strong tendency to turn her into a timeless myth instead of a human being. And so we find a very interesting combination of obvious and subtle humour in a phrase like the following: " I'm glad to see a parapidge in case of fire, and lots of roofs and chimney pots to walk upon." The obvious humour lies in the absurdity of a fat, gin-sodden old woman moving like an acrobat over the roofs of London. But the subtlety lies in the fact that by this time we have come to accept Mrs. Gamp as a praeternatural reality, freed from mortality and from the limitations of time and space. The idea of her being threatened by fire is therefore absurd. In her mythic capacity, we feel, she would not need parapidges; she would take the wings of the morning, and fly into the uttermost parts of the sea.

And so it is that the joke has an extra depth, like the jokes of Justice Shallow; an achievement which few have equalled.

Also in *Martin Chuzzlewit*, we have Pecksniff, a curious
transitional comic type, who will help us to understand why
the positive Dickensian humour was soon to be muted, and
finally disappeared altogether.   Pecksniff, unlike Mrs.
Gamp, is essential to the book's central action. He is con-
ceived mainly as a typical representative of a moral vice,
hypocrisy. To this extent, he clearly belongs to what I have
called the negative comic tradition. For a time he maintains
this character very well.

> " You will excuse Thomas Pinch's want of polish,
> Martin," said Mr. Pecksniff with a smile of patronage
> and pity. . . . " He means well."
> " He is a very good fellow, sir."
> " Oh, yes," said Mr. Pecksniff. " Yes. Thomas Pinch
> means well. He is very grateful. I have never regretted
> having befriended Thomas Pinch."

This is serious satire; and the tone of the man modestly
boasting about his non-existent virtues is very well caught.
When he says, " My daughters' room. A poor first-floor
to us, but a bower to them. Very neat. Very airy. Plants,
you observe—hyacinths; books again; birds," he seems to
be departing a little from this character. But the case is
doubtful, for this sort of whimsy is perhaps characteristic of
the sentimentalism of the utterly selfish. But only a few
pages later, he says, " There are a cart-load of loose bricks,
and a score or two of old flower-pots, in the back-yard. If
you could pile them up, my dear Martin, into any form
which would remind me on my return, say of St. Peter's in
Rome, or the Mosque of St. Sophia at Constantinople, it
would be at once improving to you and agreeable to my

feelings." Now there can be no doubt. Making allowance for a difference of class and education, we are back in Mrs. Gamp's world. And in the end, Pecksniff speaks almost in her very voice: " I wouldn't have believed it, if a fiery serpent had proclaimed it from the top of Salisbury Cathedral. I would have said that serpent lied. Such was my faith in Thomas Pinch, that I would have cast the falsehood back into the serpent's teeth, and would have taken Thomas to my heart."

Mr. Pecksniff, in fact, hovers uncertainly between positive and negative humour. He is still funny, but in an uncomfortable way, as if brilliant flashes could not compensate for the loss of inner coherence. Dickens was to move on to something as complete and satisfying as Mrs. Gamp, but at the opposite pole. A figure like Bounderby in *Hard Times* is the perfect satisfaction of those satirical gifts, which were immaturely attempting to analyse Pecksniff's hypocrisy. Bounderby is rooted in his social context; he is a profound psychological study; he is everything almost that Mrs. Gamp is not. But, though he is absurd, he is not funny.

Perhaps an occasional passage can be found in which Dickens achieved a successful harmony of his fantastic and his satirical tendencies. One, I think, is the discussion of the decline of drama in Chapter 24 of *Nicholas Nickleby*. " Mr. Curdle coughed and considered. ' The unities, Sir,' he said, ' are a completeness—a kind of a universal dovetailedness with regard to place and time—a sort of a general oneness, if I may be allowed to use so strong an expression.' " The whole chapter is gloriously absurd, extremely funny, and yet it has a satirical bite, so that all of us who indulge in the practice of literary criticism feel inclined to blush for ourselves and our colleagues.

Such perfect "dovetailedness" of very divergent gifts is,

however, rare; and it is natural that many should regret the change from Dickens the pure humourist to Dickens the satirist. But it is doubtful whether the irresponsible type of pure or positive humour in which he excelled can be indefinitely developed. And contrary tendencies, equally important in him, were all the time driving him away from it: his sense of fact, his awareness of the corporate nature of society, his psychological insight. His sense of fact and love of detail can indeed be discerned in a topsy-turvy form even in Mrs. Gamp. For, as George Orwell pointed out, we know more about Mrs. Harris, her friend who does not even exist than we do of the leading characters of some novelists. But his sense of society, and his sense of morality were bound to conflict with "positive" humour.

In Dickens's mind fantasy fought against detailed reality, and reality won after a long struggle. Gay irresponsibility fought against moral seriousness, and seriousness won eventually. Once we have this clue of the clash between different aspects of his mind, we can begin to answer the question, " What happened to Dickens's humour? " In Mrs. Gamp fantasy was in control, and detail was subordinated, emerging only in odd scraps of information about Mrs. Harris's imaginary life. In Micawber, as in Pecksniff, we have an intermediate stage where fantasy, perhaps against the author's will, is still dominant, but where an attempt is made at a moral evaluation of his perpetual borrowing and his insane hopefulness. A good many years later, Mrs. General, the governess in the Dorrit family, with her "prunes and prism," and her stiff matrimonial schemes would be a perfect subject for fantastic humour in his earlier vein. Instead we find a deadly, exact portrait (satirical, and, in the best sense, negative), of a woman for whom the details of polite behaviour have devoured their own basis and meaning in human life and affection. Best of all, in the scene where she gets her salary raised, we have an exact comment on the psychology of the type of refinement which cannot acknowledge the existence of money.

Another interesting development may be called the resultant of the clash between Dickens's amazing sense of comic eccentricity, and his ultimately powerful, but slowly-developing, sense of society. The early eccentrics can afford to ignore society. To ask how Pickwick managed to succeed in business and make his fortune would be a meaningless question. The sorrows of Dick Swiveller are only, as it were, the low notes in his incomparable personal song. There is no real pressure of society; but gradually Dickens came to set his eccentrics against society, and to examine the tensions and potential tragedies of the relationship. An early, melodramatic, but still hauntingly impressive example is Quilp. A late, melancholy example is John Rokesmith, whose oddness and loneliness are due to the provisions of a will, the power of money, and the customs of society, more than to his own personality. A magnificent and profound later example is Mr. Dorrit, every corner of whose mind is modified by the experience of being a gentleman in prison; and another is the heir of *Great Expectations*. All these achievements required in their author a sense of the fantastic eccentricity of people. As his comic exuberance declined, his comic gifts were not wasted, but transformed.

3

The Expanding Prison

The paramount importance of prisons in Dickens's imaginative life hardly needs to be demonstrated. It is not merely that his father was imprisoned for debt, and that four or five of his books deal with the subject at length, while several others treat it more briefly. Without any biographical reconstructions or laborious statistical statements, every attentive reader is aware that the prison is a dominating image in his work. With the possible exception of Stendhal, there is no other distinguished novelist in whose work the idea is so important.

We are aware of this not only in *Little Dorrit*, where the old Marshalsea dominates the whole action; it is perhaps even more significant that the idea keeps creeping into passages in other novels, where it seems scarcely relevant. For example, in *The Old Curiosity Shop* Little Nell's grandfather is afraid of being forcibly separated from her. This is how the fear presents itself to his mind:

> They will shut me up in a stone room, dark and cold, and chain me up to the wall, Nell, flog me with whips.

He has committed no crime, but for many of Dickens's characters, as for the author himself, the image of the prison is always waiting to well up into the mind in moments of crisis. Similarly, other institutions, such as dark and forbidding houses, or workhouses, or schools readily acquire the prison atmosphere. Even voluntary prisoners like Clennam's mother and Miss Havisham may develop all the mental characteristics of people confined by force; and the invisible bonds may be more permanent than the prison walls which sometimes, as in the case of Mr. Dorrit, admit of release.

Several books move between the poles of two kinds of imprisonment as if to suggest that there is ultimately no escape. *Oliver Twist* begins with the "charitable" workhouse imprisonment of Oliver, and ends with Fagin's condemned cell. *A Tale of Two Cities* begins with a royalist prison and ends with a revolutionary one. In *Little Dorrit* this simple idea of the return of the prison is treated with greater subtlety until the prison seems to be everywhere.

Most people are unfamiliar with prisons and are content to have a few simplified, stock ideas about them: for instance, that prisons are necessary but pathetic, or that they are in need of reform and improvement. Dickens's response is naturally much more complex, and more difficult to analyse. But there is one cardinal divergence from the usual attitudes. In reading Dickens we are always seeing the prison from the inside. The primary thing is never the prison as a legal enactment, or a social problem, but an experience, which we are compelled to share. Apparent exceptions only confirm this point, as when Little Dorrit is locked out of the Marshalsea. She is locked out of her home, and so spends the night more aware than usual of the fact that she belongs nowhere else. As has often been recalled, the debtors' prison had ceased to exist when *Little Dorrit* was written, just as the hulks had disappeared when *Great Expectations* was written. Neither book is an essay in social reform. Both are concerned with the nature of a prisoner's experience.

Even in the very early *Sketches by Boz* there is a visit to Newgate; but the first significant version of the prison image occurs in *Pickwick Papers*, which, as everybody knows, is the embodiment of a genuine and important, but not very profound aspect of Dickens's nature—the clownish, jolly, vulgar, superficially generous. Even if the prison was a dominating idea for him, he might have been expected to ignore it for once. He did not do that, but he allowed it to appear in deceptive and unreal guise. Mr. Pickwick's imprisonment is, in almost every respect, the opposite of normal. He goes to prison voluntarily, because he refuses on principle to pay damages that are too small to impair his fortune. While he is there he lives in luxury, is comfortable, and is able to occupy himself as he likes. He is not disgraced, but is admired for his fortitude; he retains the affection of his friends and the disinterested loyalty of his servant. He is not required to mingle with the wretched, dirty and poverty-stricken prisoners on the "other side," but when he decides out of pure kindness to go among them for a time, he witnesses, but without any vengeful feelings, the degradation of his old enemy, Jingle. He pities and patronises the wretched, and even, at one point, most improbably of all (for he has led a sheltered life and is old and fat) holds his own in physical combat with a younger man. Finally, after a short period of imprisonment, he is able to secure release while maintaining his dignity, and to take pity on his unjust accuser. In fact, Mr. Pickwick's imprisonment is a kind of triumphal progress, a vast moral victory gained at very little cost. And all this, of course, is just what we should expect. The whole book is written in a kind of euphoria; the dangers and pains and difficulties of life are no more than a humorous and exhilarating obstacle race in which ultimate success is certain. But one may, in such a euphoric mood, feel compelled to recall former fears and worries, to prove to oneself how easily one can now conquer them. So the appearance of the prison here, though it is only a prison physically and not psychologically, is still significant. The prison in *Pickwick Papers* represents an early and false attempt to scotch what would afterwards prove to be an intractable preoccupation. In the context of Dickens's whole career the gay prison scenes in it are very sad. Dickens was in the position of a drunken debtor outlining his brilliant plans for making a fortune.

In *Oliver Twist*, written a year or two later, a new, but still unsatisfactory attempt is made upon the problem. Oliver's birth in the workhouse, which has sufficiently grim implications, is partly shuffled off with the uneasy facetiousness of passages like this:

Although I am not disposed to maintain that the being born in a workhouse is in itself the most fortunate and enviable circumstance that can possibly befall a human being, I do mean to say that in this particular instance, it was the best thing for Oliver Twist that could possibly have occurred. The fact is, that there was considerable difficulty in inducing Oliver to take upon himself the office of respiration—a troublesome practice, but one which custom has rendered necessary to our easy existence; and for some time he lay gasping. . . . Now if, during this brief period, Oliver had been surrounded by careful grandmothers, anxious aunts, experienced nurses, and doctors of profound wisdom, he would most inevitably and indubitably have been killed in no time. There being nobody by, however, but a pauper old woman, who was rendered rather misty by an unwonted allowance of beer; and a parish surgeon who did such matters by contract; Oliver and nature fought the point between them.

This passage occurs in the book's third paragraph, and it shows straight away that Dickens has not settled his own attitude to his subject. To describe a lonely boy's unhappy childhood in this tone throughout would be heartless and superficial. But, of course, the tone rapidly changes, and afterwards oscillates between this facetiousness and a pathos that tends to a blurred, exaggerated effect. The origin of both tones is probably the same. They spring from a too close personal identification with his hero. In his attitude to his own troubles Dickens could be secretive, blustering and anxious to keep up respectable appearances; this would correspond to the passage quoted. He could also be expansively self-pitying, as in his autobiographical account of the blacking factory; and this would correspond to the more pathetic scenes in *Oliver Twist*.

The foregoing account may seem rather severe. Wouldn't we all be given to self-pity if we had shared Dickens's childhood experiences? No doubt; but it seems to me that the indulgence and sympathy properly accorded to the man is not properly accorded to the novelist. It is against Dickens as artist only, not as man that we can justly make these criticisms, especially as they only serve to throw into relief his final artistic triumph, in *Little Dorrit*, over this fascinating and intractable material.

The emotional incoherence of the author, at this stage, is very obviously reflected in Oliver himself. He is at one moment a snivelling child, and at another a formidable delinquent and home worker. At other times again he is not very far from being a polished man of the world:

" And consider, ma'am," said Oliver, as the tears forced themselves into his eyes, despite his efforts to the contrary :

" oh! consider how young and good she is, and what pleasure and comfort she gives to all about her. I am sure —certain—quite certain—that, for your sake, who are so good yourself, and for her own; for the sake of all she makes so happy; she will not die. Heaven will never let her die so young."

It is obvious from passages like this that no serious thought has been given to the practical effects of being educated in a workhouse and a thieves' kitchen. And the failure is particularly startling if one remembers Dickens's habitual mastery of strange popular idioms—in Mrs. Gamp, for instance, and Sam Weller. And so, though gloomier and outwardly more authentic than in *Pickwick Papers*, the prison remains psychologically unreal.

On the other hand, no one would call *Oliver Twist* a falsely cheerful book. It conveys an impression of horror which every reader remembers when he may have forgotten most of the details. This horror is largely unexplained; the stagy plot is inadequate to it. The book is like a continuous and unsuccessful attempt to pin down, externalise and face the overwhelming nightmares of childhood. And of course the attempt ends in a prison.

The account of Fagin in the condemned cell is certainly vivid and memorable and it is not easy to say just what is wrong with it. But a clue may be found in such a passage as this:

" The dreadful walls of Newgate, which have hidden so much misery and such unspeakable anguish, not only from the eyes, but, too often, and too long from the thoughts, of men, never held so dread a spectacle as that." i.e. as Fagin sitting alone. This solitary reference to the misery and anguish of Newgate is perfunctory, and is, in any case, out of key with its context, for this prison is presented neither as a social problem nor as a symbol, but as a just punishment of evil. Fagin ceases to be a recognisable member of the criminal class, and becomes a kind of hellish scapegoat. (Cruickshank's famous drawing, in which the condemned Fagin does not look human at all, is entirely in the spirit of the text.) The problem of his guilt, the tricky concepts of crime and punishment are shelved, and instead his execution provides a rather cheap catharsis, a thrill followed by peace. It is almost as if the world's evil falters when the master of evil is killed. If *Pickwick Papers* offers us the prison as quite a jolly place after all, here we have the prison as necessary for the control of vermin. And there is an element of dishonesty in this for the deep thrill derived from contemplating the punishment is not admitted. It only serves to obscure at the end the book's deepest preoccupation—the irrational fears of childhood.

II

In *Barnaby Rudge* and in *A Tale of Two Cities* Dickens caused two of the dominating images of his literary life to clash. The crowd makes war on the prison. In these passages we are aware of a very deep excitement in the author, as if this was his own private version of the meeting of irresistible force and immovable object. Leaving *Barnaby* for further discussion in the chapter on crowds, I turn now to the prisons of *A Tale of Two Cities*. If examined in association with *Oliver Twist*, the prison chapters here read almost like a reply to the superficiality of Fagin's death scene. If prison is only the temporary detention of the innocent boy, who is sure to be saved in the end, or the horrible but just punishment of the thoroughly evil man, much of its terror disappears. But in *A Tale of Two Cities* it is a great deal more than this. Manette has been released from " 105 North Tower," the royalist prison, and is living in the house of the revolutionary plotter, Defarge. He is free, but his freedom means nothing to him. He is always alone, and can scarcely bear visitors. He requires to be locked in his room, " because he has lived so long locked up, that he would be frightened—rave, tear himself to pieces —die—come to I know not what harm, if his door was left open."

He has forgotten his name, but remembers perpetually the number of his prison room, and he still occupies himself with the manual work he did in prison. But worse, he has not only forgotten himself as a human being, he has been virtually forgotten by his benefactors. Defarge does not pity him as a kind of dead trophy or example to stir up revolutionary feeling. So influential is Defarge's view of him that it momentarily infects even Defarge's daughter.

> " I am afraid of it."
> " Of it? Of what? "
> " I mean of him . . . of my father."

We miss the point if we read this merely as a description of callous perversity. On the contrary, when the prisoner is described by the author, he appears in much the same light. " He, and his old canvas frock, and his loose stockings, and all his poor tatters of clothes, had, in a long seclusion from direct light and air, faded down to such a dull uniformity of parchment-yellow, that it would have been hard to say which was which." Here is Dickens's ultimate in misery, a suffering that cannot be relieved, pitied or understood, that is not aware of itself, and to the question " I hope you care to be recalled to life? " can only answer " I can't say."

And to make us universalise the picture, and apply it to

the suffering world in general, Dickens placed at the end of the chapter this image: " Beneath that arch of unmoved and eternal lights; some, so remote from this little earth that the learned tell us it is doubtful whether their rays have even yet discovered it, as a point in space where anything is suffered or done. . . ."

In this chapter, Dickens achieved something new. He used the image of the prison for a steady gaze, without self-pity or hysteria, at the general miseries of life. For although Manette can recover his wits and his human dignity, the prison is lurking within him, ready to regain control, when a new emotional crisis occurs. At the time of his daughter's marriage he goes back to his unconscious shoemaking. Perhaps this incident has a somewhat unreal and contrived air. But its importance in the author's development is nevertheless considerable. Dickens was, as we have seen, exceptionally aware of external objects; his imagination was extraordinarily literal; his psychological grasp, which was eventually to become formidable, was slow to develop. His natural tendency, therefore, was to blame all the misery he observed on circumstances, on tyrants, on social conditions. So it was bound to take time for him to comprehend that the prison he was endlessly seeking to describe and understand was, in part, the mental creation of the prisoner, that to strike away the chains and fetters could not solve all the prisoner's problems. Having now realised this, having arrived at his own version of the discovery:

" O the mind, mind has mountains; cliffs of fall
   Frightful, sheer, no-man fathomed."

he was eventually able to develop it in the case of Miss Havisham into a deep psychological study.

But it may be objected that all this special pleading does not improve the quality of the actual scene in which Manette returns to his shoemaking, if, as I have suggested, that is deficient. And, of course, that is true. Dickens was, in his way, a great artist, but he was never a pure artist. Aspects of his mind, interesting in themselves, but structurally irrelevant, are always liable to break in. But sometimes, as here, we can have the satisfaction of feeling that the imperfections contribute to the making of later and better works.

The consequences of Manette's hopeless misery are very instructive. When the Revolution comes, his long years of imprisonment under the old régime entitle Manette to a privileged position. He can use his influence on behalf of his accused son-in-law; and he can even say " It all tended to a good end, my friend; it was not mere waste and ruin." When these hopes seem to be fulfilled, he is a proud and happy man. But the release of Evremonde is only temporary. He is once again denounced and sentenced to death. The melodramatic ending in which Evremonde is saved by the substitution of Carton, cannot obscure the significance of this. For Evremonde's second condemnation is occasioned by the reading of a document written by Manette in prison. The supposed utility of those long years in prison ends in disillusionment. And at this point, with sombre appropriateness, Manette returns, as Dorrit had done so much more convincingly, to the imbecile mode of consciousness which possessed him in his prison years.

So the direct and tangible value of prisoners' suffering is implicitly denied. But there is still a strange dignity in the prison, which comes to Evremonde as a surprise:

" In the instinctive association of prisoners with shameful crimes and disgrace, the newcomer recoiled from his company. But the crowning unreality of his long unreal ride, was, their all at once rising to receive him, with every refinement of manner known to the time, and with all the engaging graces and courtesies of life."

No doubt Dickens had read of some such scene in the French Revolution, but all the same, this dignity had personal significance also for him. It reduces the prison to a terror of manageable proportions. If it cannot be called a complete moral or artistic answer to the problem of the prison which he carried with him through his writing life, it at least contains no cheat or deception. He was making progress.

III

For a book completely dominated by the prison image we turn, of course, to *Little Dorrit*. And if this is one of the greatest English novels of the nineteenth century, it is partly because a writer of matchless gifts and also of grave short-comings here for the first time explores in depth the subject of his deepest obsession. Dickens at last squarely faces both the social problem and the personal problem and makes ample amends for previous evasions, inconsistencies and imaginative failures.

Little Dorrit begins with the prison at Marseilles. " In Marseilles that day there was a villainous prison. In one of its chambers, so repulsive a place that even the obtrusive stars blinked at it, and left it to such refuse of reflected light as it could find for itself, were two men. Besides the two men, a notched and disfigured bench, immovable from the wall, with a draught-board rudely hacked upon it with a knife, a set of draughts, made of old buttons and soup bones, a set of dominoes, two mats, and two or three wine bottles. That was all the chamber held, exclusive of rats and other unseen vermin, in addition to the seen vermin, the two men."

Vermin—it is a terrible word to apply to men. And our first feeling may be to reject it angrily, to ask ourselves if that is what all Dickens's fine humane sentiments and generous impulses to reform have come to at last. We may remind ourselves bitterly that these two men are foreigners, that Dickens was influenced by many stupid John Bull-ish prejudices. There is some truth in all these complaints. But they partly miss the point. For one of the two prisoners, Blandois is diabolical. He has just enough character to be credible, and to play rather a stagy part in the plot. But his chief function is to represent the mystery of iniquity, and to remind us at the same time that " The Prince of darkness is a gentleman." Although in prison on a charge of murder, he exacts service from his companion. He will not soil his hands with work. As Lionel Trilling bluntly and truly says, " Because Blandois exists, prisons are necessary." He ensures that we never forget this while we read of the terrible and useless sufferings imposed by the other prison, the Marshalsea. The other piece of human vermin, though technically guilty of an offence against the law, is a man of exemplary kindness, humility and patience. Why is he described as vermin? The answer to this fundamental question appears only very gradually as the book proceeds. Society, finding prisons to be necessary, because Blandois exists, herds good men and bad into them and treats them all as outcasts. But vermin means primarily parasitic creatures. And this is, in a way, a true description of both good and bad. Both are outside society, one because the gentleman's code forbids him to co-operate with society by work, the other because he cannot find work to do, because society has refused him a livelihood. Both must therefore live, one voluntarily, the other involuntarily upon the fruits of the labour of others. In this brief, schematic opening scene we are presented straight away with the prisoner who is too bad for society and the prisoner who is too good for society.

The next version of the prison in *Little Dorrit* is the temporary confinement in which the Meagles family, Clennam and others are kept by the quarantine laws. This is mainly a device for throwing together some of the book's characters, but it does contribute something. For Mr. Meagles says, on his release, " ' But I bear those monotonous walls no ill-will now. One always forgives a place as soon as it's left behind; I dare say a prisoner begins to relent towards his prison, after he is let out.' "

Meagles is an ordinary man who has momentarily shared a small part of the prisoners' experience, and he represents the average unimaginative opinion that prison is merely a temporary confinement without lasting effects. In fact, every other prisoner in the book (and that includes, in one way or another, most of its characters), is a striking refutation of Meagles's good-natured statement. We might say that Meagles says what Dickens himself might have said at the time of *Pickwick Papers*. But now he knew better, and soon he shows us Arthur Clennam's mother, one of a series of voluntary prisoners, in order to drive home the point. It is useless to try to release such a woman from the bondage of a single room. There is nowhere for her to go.

Finally, we arrive at the subtlest and greatest of all Dickens's prisons—the Marshalsea. For a man of keen sensitivity to ridicule and disgrace, and one must add, however unwillingly, of formidable concealed snobbery, it was something of a triumph to write at length about the prison in which his father had been confined, and in which he himself spent so many Sundays as a child. The emotions aroused by these memories do not directly appear in *Little Dorrit*. The passing of many years had enabled him to

eliminate personal shame and anger; yet his personal
feelings survive in a strangely transmuted form. The first
description of the Marshalsea is curiously nostalgic; and we
soon find that the place possesses an attraction for its
inmates. It is a place of rest, of kindness, of gentle and
harmless deceit.

When Mrs. Dorrit is giving birth there, the charwoman
says, " ' The flies trouble you, don't they, my dear? But
p'r'aps they'll take your mind off it, and do you good. What
between the buryin' ground, the grocer's, the waggon-
stables, and the paunch trade, the Marshalsea flies gets very
large. P'r'aps they're sent as a consolation, if we only
know'd it.' " The religious sensibility revealed here may not
be of a very high order, but the humanity and kindness are
genuine. In the same scene the beery, disreputable doctor
says: " ' We are quiet here; we don't get badgered here;
there's no knocker here, sir, to be hammered at by creditors
and bring a man's heart into his mouth. Nobody comes here
to ask if a man's at home, and to say he'll stand on the
door mat till he is. Nobody writes threatening letters
about money to this place. It's freedom, sir, it's freedom.' "

But it is precisely this peace, this freedom and kindness
which prove to be the gravest dangers. They destroy Mr.
Dorrit by nourishing a temperament naturally subject to
genteel illusions. The flattery of the turnkey, the homage
of the other prisoners are a kind of siren song. However far
he travels after his release, he remains spiritually an in-
habitant of the Marshalsea, and it is appropriate that just
before his death he should return to his old way of speaking,
and patronise his brother in the same style as he once
patronised his "pensioner" Nandy.

And the effect on the next generation is greater still. They
are at their mildest, of course, in Little Dorrit herself. She

retains all her life an attachment to the prison, which is partly due to the memory of having useful work to do, and of living without false grandeur, but is also no doubt partly a morbid regression. There is a certain symbolical force as well as a more conventional pathos in the scene where she is shut out of the Marshalsea at night, and crouches as near as she can to the locked gate. More important still is the scene in which she asks Clennam whether it is just that her father, who is now rich, should pay the ancient debts for which he had been imprisoned so long.

" Mr. Clennam, will he pay all his debts before he leaves here? "

" No doubt. All."

" All the debts for which he has been imprisoned here, all my life and longer? "

" No doubt."

There was something of uncertainty and remonstrance in her look; something that was not all satisfaction. He wondered to detect it, and said: " You are glad that he should do so? "

" Are you? " asked Little Dorrit, wistfully.

" Am I? Most heartily glad! "

" Then I know I ought to be."

" And are you not? "

" It seems to me hard," said Little Dorrit, " that he should have lost so many years and suffered so much, and at last pay all the debts as well. It seems to me hard that he should pay in life and money both."

" My dear child . . ." Clennam was beginning.

" Yes, I know I am wrong," she pleaded timidly, " don't think any worse of me; it has grown up with me here."

The prison which could spoil so many things, had tainted Little Dorrit no more than this.

This unobtrusive little scene seems to me to be one of Dickens's greatest triumphs. In this girl, pattern of responsibility as she is, this slight taint of irresponsibility has appeared. Debts now seem to her to be a natural handicap for which life exacts a terrible penalty. The idea of debt as something really owed has become unreal to her. It is beyond her imagination that the creditor also might have suffered hardship through unpaid debts. In the final comment by the author just quoted there is implied a terrible *a fortiori*. In the case of her brother the stain appears first as financial improvidence copied from his elders, and then as a general moral irresponsibility. In her sister it appears as an implacable desire to assert the family's social superiority. Later when the family is rich and respected, she feels it necessary to take vengeance, through a meaningless marriage, upon the people who dared to patronise her when she was poor.

Among the ordinary inhabitants of the Marshalsea, insolvency comes to be regarded as the natural condition of man, and the payment of debts as a disease which occasionally breaks out. (We realise with a shock that this bizarre attitude is also a logical development of Little Dorrit's slight haziness of mind about her father's debts.) And crowning all is Mr. Dorrit's superb sense of the benefits he has conferred on the fellow-prisoners who had the privilege of paying for his comforts. As the time of his release approaches, " Mr. Dorrit, yielding to the vast speculation how the poor creatures were to get on without him, was great, and sad, but not absorbed. He patted children on the head like Sir Roger de Coverley going to church, he spoke to people in the background by their Christian names, he condescended to all present, and seemed for their consolation to walk encircled by the legend in golden characters, ' Be comforted, my people! Bear it! ' "

When we find so many people in the Marshalsea hugging their chains, and paying such homage to the prisoner of longest standing, it is no surprise to find in the book other voluntary prisons. Mrs. Clennam has voluntarily confined herself to a single room to atone for the imprisonment of the Dorrits for which she is responsible. It is interesting to notice that this is not held to her credit by the author. It is presented as the subtlest kind of self-indulgence and self-deception. She gives up movement, the pleasures of the senses and of friendship, because she does not, in the last resort, really care for them. She refuses to give up the two things she really cares for, the sacrifice of which the situation really demands, her money and her reputation for righteousness. Her imprisonment thus becomes an outward expression of her gloomy and terrible religion, which is paradoxically the product of self-indulgence and wish-fulfilment. In his account of her actual doctrines Dickens was, as so often in his discussions of religion, superficial. But the conception of her voluntary imprisonment as a deceptive, unreal and ineffective penance, concealing from her mind the duty to make amends to the injured, has great imaginative truth. And once again it is a shock to realise that it is an infinitely grimmer version of the imaginative failure of Little Dorrit herself. It, too, embodies the idea, " Why should debts be paid in money if they have been paid in suffering? " To present this key idea in such startlingly different garbs, to reveal the similarity and the difference, to reserve this kindly severity for a favourite heroine, and to do it all easily and naturally, all this, surely is the work of a great artist.

It is very much in accord with the book's dominant tone,

that the Dorrits, when released, should immediately exchange the Marshalsea for the dreary confinement of the hotel at the top of the Alps. When Dorrit complains of the atmosphere of confinement, the innkeeper tells him that " Monsieur could not easily place himself in the position of a person who had not the power to choose, I will go here to-morrow or there next day; I will pass these barriers, I will enlarge these bounds. Monsieur could not realise, perhaps, how the mind accommodated itself in such things to the force of necessity."

The irony of this is that it is the spiritually free man who is pointing out to the imprisoned the unlimited, but for him unreal, advantages of his wealth and freedom of movement. Mr. Dorrit imagines that the prison is only a kind of guilty secret which he must prevent other people from finding out. He does not see any connection between the old life and the new. He does not realise that the same impulse which led him to patronise Nandy will later lead him to patronise his dying brother. It is left to the more clear-sighted Little Dorrit herself to realise that their new fashionable life is also a prison. " It appeared on the whole to Little Dorrit herself, that this same society in which they lived, greatly resembled a superior sort of Marshalsea. Numbers of people seemed to come abroad, pretty much as people had come into prison; through debt, through idleness, relationship, curiosity, and general unfitness for getting on at home." This parallel is extended in detail, some of which is unconvincing. But the fundamental point, which is essential to the book's whole conception, is that a man can travel everywhere and carry his prison within him.

When Clennam eventually returns to the Marshalsea, not as a visitor, as in the past, but as a prisoner, this vision is endorsed and extended by the author himself. " The last day of the appointed week touched the bars of the Marshalsea gate. Black, all night, since the gate had clashed upon Little Dorrit, its iron stripes were turned by the early-glowing sun into stripes of gold. For aslant across the city over its jumbled roofs, and through the open tracery of its church towers, struck the long bright rays, bars of the prison of this lower world."

The technical failure involved here is discussed in the chapter on *Little Dorrit*. Here we may notice the immensely powerful drive, over-powerful, even clumsy in its operation perhaps, to impose the prison symbol on society. The fact that the debtors' prison no longer existed when *Little Dorrit* was written served Dickens's purpose in two ways. It gave poignancy to the curious, sickly and deceptive nostalgia with which the prison is treated. And by ruling out any suggestion of reforming zeal or complaint, by inhibiting the reaction, " Get rid of the prison and all will be well," it enabled him to give added force to the idea. " You have destroyed the prison, but it is, of course, in its essence, indestructible." Or " You have destroyed it only to make it spread, until it envelops you all." The ghost of the prison is thus more powerful than the former reality.

Yet in this vision of the world, with all its gloom, its determinism, and even perhaps its cruelty there is a hint of hope contained in those bars of sunlight and that " lower world." What of the upper world? Dickens could never do more than hint at this. But the hint seems to bear fruit in the final marriage of Clennam and Little Dorrit at the prison gate, i.e. perhaps on the road to heaven. If this last part of the book seems to be in danger of breaking down under the weight of symbols, and if probability is sacrificed, it is a sign, no doubt that the symbols were of crucial importance to the author.

In the long line of Dickens's attempts to exorcise the prison obsession, *Little Dorrit* is the subtlest and most

artistically fruitful. But it may be that this one, too, has its
unsatisfactory side. If *Pickwick Papers* shows the prison
made impossibly lighthearted and tolerable, and *Oliver Twist*
shows a prison justified by the satanic wickedness of the men
in it, *Little Dorrit* adds the idea of the prison spreading out-
wards to cover everything. Dickens often writes like a man
anticipating the objections of an unseen audience. (See, for
instance, the vehemently defensive tone of so many of his
introductions.) Here it is almost as if he is countering the
imagined sneer, " You're a prison boy, your father was in
prison," with the retort, " You're all in prison but you don't
know it." The frightening thing about *Little Dorrit* is that
it gives almost no scope to the freedom of the will. It is a
book full of travelling, but no one can choose not to go
continually from one prison to another. Little Dorrit
oscillates between the Clennam house and the Marshalsea.
Blandois escapes from one prison, only to perish with over-
neat symbolical effect by the collapse of the house where
Mrs. Clennam has made an abiding prison for herself.
Brilliant and intensely alive as the prison is in *Little Dorrit*,
certain technical faults point to deeper uncertainties. You
do not necessarily solve a problem by making it universal.
In the deepening universality of his vision Dickens made no
real attempt on the question, " How shall we live in the
prison ? "

IV

In its treatment of prisons as in other ways too, *Great
Expectations*, perhaps the most subtle and elusive of Dickens's
books, is hard to classify. In the first place we have another,
a more Gothic, more memorable, more sympathetic version,
of the self-imposed imprisonment of Mrs. Clennam.
" I saw that the bride within the bridal dress had withered

like the dress, and like the flowers, and had no brightness
left but the brightness of her sunken eyes. I saw that the
dress had been put upon the rounded figure of a young
woman, and that the figure upon which it now hung loose,
had shrunk to skin and bone. Once, I had been taken to
some ghastly waxworks at the Fair, representing I know not
what impossible personage lying in state. Once, I had been
taken to one of our old marsh churches to see a skeleton in
the ashes of a rich dress, that had been dug out of a vault
under the church pavement. Now waxwork and skeleton
seemed to have dark eyes that moved and looked at me."
Unlike Mrs. Clennam and Mr. Dorrit and nearly all
Dickens's other prisoners she is primarily someone who is
seen. Her own mode of consciousness remains largely
obscure. The word "waxwork" is significant, and it recurs
in another context.

> While I looked about me here [Newgate prison], an
> exceedingly dirty and partially drunk minister of justice
> asked me if I would like to step in and hear a trial or so;
> informing me that he could give me a front place for half-
> a-crown, whence I should command a full view of the
> Lord Chief Justice in his wig and robes—mentioning
> that awful personage like wax-work, and presently offer-
> ing him at the reduced price of eighteenpence.

What do these two passages have in common? In each
case Pip imagines he is a detached spectator, that he can
treat a new aspect of life as if it were a waxwork show. In
each case he is really about to be deeply involved. And this
is perhaps the key to the treatment of the prison in *Great
Expectations*. It is no longer a dominant image casting long
shadows on every part of the book. It is a fertile soil out of
which things grow for the delight or the profit or the
undoing of people who have never thought about this soil.

A convict is the author of Pip's good fortune, but Pip will be horrified when he knows this. The incident in chapter eighteen (an improbable one if taken literally), of Pip travelling in the stage coach with the convicts, is no doubt meant to suggest the idea, "All in the same boat." In *Little Dorrit* you could escape the prison but not forget it. Here you can ignore it but you cannot escape it. All Pip's wealth comes from the convict, and so does Estella. The satire upon Pip's genteel shame and horror are like Dickens's delayed self-punishment for his own. The situation is only made more intolerable by the fact that the convict for all his vulgar dreams of gentlemanliness, is lovable. Pip painfully helps him to escape—he gives him the help which Dickens perhaps failed to give his own father.

" I consumed the whole time in thinking how strange it was that I should be encompassed by all this taint of prison and crime; that in my childhood out on our lonely marshes on a winter evening I should have first encountered it; that, it should have reappeared on two occasions, starting out like a stain that was faded but not gone; that it should in this new way pervade my fortune and advancement." In these words of Pip, Dickens expressed one of the great enigmas of his own life, one which it took him many years to comprehend. And, he expressed it here, perhaps for the first time clearly and simply, without elaboration or distortion. In such a case the simplest and clearest statement was the most difficult of all to achieve.

It is difficult to sum up in a matter of such complexity. From one point of view Dickens's prolonged attack upon the subject may be seen as a struggle to find value, even usefulness in the prison experience. First melodramatically, as in *Oliver Twist*, and then more seriously in the case of Blandois in *Little Dorrit* the prison is useful because it is necessary for the protection of society, and the restraint of wickedness. But Dickens really knew very well that this idea, whether true or not, was not the solution he was searching for. For one thing, it could not explain why the subject gripped his imagination. Then he tried to think of the suffering and confinement of prisoners as positively beneficial in their future lives. This concept seems for a time to govern the plot of *A Tale of Two Cities*. Manette's imprisonment apparently gives him the right, under a new revolutionary régime, to prevent the persecution of those he loves.

But one of the reasons why Dickens, even when not at his best, is such an interesting writer, is that his plots have a life of their own. There are frequent conflicts between the rational planning mind of the artist and a kind of hidden subconscious logic possessed by the story itself. Perhaps as the result of some such conflict, Manette's power to influence events proves to be an illusion; this signifies the impossibility, at this stage, of believing that the prison will be the cause of happiness.

But in the universal prisons of *Little Dorrit* and *Great Expectations*, we seem to detect in the author a despairing satisfaction in the idea that the prison is everywhere, is unavoidable, and is, like life itself, an inextricable mixture of pleasure and pain. It would seem that the prison became for Dickens emblematic of the whole problem of suffering. The man was so practical that he had to struggle to solve this problem in terms of necessary sacrifice for future progress and happiness in life. With one part of his mind at least, he approached the prison in a matter-of-fact, almost hedonistic vein. Such an attempt must fail. And so Dickens has really nothing to tell us about how to live in prison. Perhaps prudently he evaded the most difficult task of all. It is no use complaining that Dickens was not Dostoevsky.

But what he did, he did superbly. He presented an immense range of prison experience. He showed its intimate connection at every point with the lives of the free and respectable. He showed the relevance of the idea to many aspects of society, from the Bastille to the slums. He transformed personal shame and fear into art.

4

Reform and Indignation

It was characteristic of Dickens to be angry. This is a fact
which should always be remembered when we are considering his politics, his social theories, or his status as a "reformer." Good, hot, generous anger is very enjoyable to
some people; and a high proportion of distinguished
Victorians were of this type. One need only mention
Huxley, Trollope, Gladstone and Macaulay. These men
and Dickens himself differed a great deal in their opinions
and in their talents. But they had several qualities in
common. They all had superabundant energy, great versa-
tility and unfailing determination to succeed. There can be
no doubt that their anger was linked with these qualities.
It absorbed surplus energy; it helped to convince them that
their ambitions were morally justified. It toned up the
system.

All this may sound a little cynical; and it would indeed
be cynical if it was offered as a complete explanation, which
of course it is not. Their anger may often have been
justified. There was much to be angry about in 1840, as at
other times. But I do not think it is possible to understand
Dickens's satire, his criticisms of society, and his reforming
zeal, unless it is agreed that anger was for him a necessity
of life.

Now such a trait of character may be very obvious in the case of another person, as I think it is in this case. But it would require an exceptional degree of self-knowledge to make such an analysis of oneself. Perhaps few great writers have had less self-knowledge than Dickens. He had a good deal of the actor's temperament, as his friends and the public who attended his readings were well aware. He had occasional flashes of introspection, but in the main he saw himself as a public figure. The reflection of the image he presented to the public was more real to him than anything he learned about himself in the quietness of his study. If he needed any encouragement to believe that his anger was profound social insight, and reforming zeal, he soon received it from an adoring public.

Dickens's lack of self-knowledge is neatly illustrated by the history of his first American journey. The desire to visit America seized his mind with sudden fervour. In the words of Edgar Johnson, " The United States symbolised for him the goal of liberty and democracy toward which he hoped that England might be tending. It was the glowing promise of a future in which the worn-out snobberies, aristocratic privileges, and corruptions of the Old World gave way to a better scheme of things and men were valued according to their character and accomplishment. ' I am still haunted,' he wrote Forster, ' by visions of America, night and day. . . .' "

He was also displeased with the prevailing tone of English comment on American institutions, a good example of which is Mrs. Trollope's *Domestic Manners of the Americans*, and he thought of writing a counterblast to such accounts which would help to establish America as the English radicals' Mecca. As everybody knows, the literary result of his American tour, which can be studied in *American Notes* and especially in *Martin Chuzzlewit*, was very different.

The central chapters of *Martin Chuzzlewit* have some claim to be considered the most virulent that Dickens ever wrote. They are not merely angry, they are utterly contemptuous. The satirised Americans are left with scarcely a trace of common humanity. And yet, Dickens discovered no new *facts* about America. The factual basis of every complaint he makes is to be found in earlier books about America, which he had read before he left England. He may have confirmed by observation the truth of a few accusations which he had hesitated to believe. But he cannot have failed to know, before he left, of the institution of slavery or of American piracy of English copyrights—two of the things he was later to attack most bitterly. And though he may originally have supposed that Mrs. Trollope was too severe, he certainly did not believe her to be a liar. Clearly his revulsion of feeling cannot be written off simply as the natural fruit of his American observations.

Nor can we explain his ferocious reaction to America in terms of personal pique, or of quarrels, or of failure to adjust himself to American social life. For we know that his American tour was a triumphal progress. Not only was he treated everywhere as a great man, but he was well liked, and made friends. It seems that the explanation cannot lie mainly in his actual experiences in America. And no doubt it is foolish to speak as if such emotional upheavals could ever be fully explained. But it would seem that Dickens's indignation was of the kind that implies an *emotional dependence* on the people and institutions against which anger is directed. That is to say, it was (speaking very generally) of the same kind as a son's anger against a father, an officer's anger against the War Office, an Etonian's anger against the public schools. It was not in the main comparable to the idealist's rejection of compromise and corruption, or the ascetic determination to renounce the world, still less to a fanatic zeal for a perfect society. His anger, indeed, often had a strong moral basis, or rather perhaps it would be more accurate to say that it strongly associated itself with moral stimuli, but there was little, if anything, in Dickens's moral appeal that was not wholeheartedly accepted by his readers. He asked for honesty, justice and mercy; and he understood these words, just as his readers did, in terms ultimately based on Christian ethics, but intertwined with vague and sentimental concepts derived from Rousseau.

I have said that Dickens's writings show an emotional dependence on the institutions he attacked. In the chapter on *Little Dorrit* I try to show that this is so even when he deals with the debtors' prison, with which he had (through his father) such painful early associations. This is an extreme case, but many of Dickens's bitterest attacks are reminiscent of a man trying to burst through a locked door with his shoulder. If he succeeds, he is in danger of collapsing.

As a rule, this emotional dependence is not, at first, fully conscious. For instance, the adolescent son who loses no opportunity to proclaim the old-fashioned stupidity of his parents does not realise that he will feel homesick when he leaves home. He certainly does not guess that absence from home will bring into the open his latent admiration for his father. When he discovers this by experience, it will not be astonishing if he turns with redoubled ferocity against the customs of his new home; if, so to speak, he sets out to punish it for not being his old home. Something analogous to this occurred, I believe, when Dickens became a bitter critic of America.

If one studies the consequences of this, in the middle part of *Martin Chuzzlewit*, one begins to notice a difference between the old anger against England and the new anger against America. In his earlier works at least, Dickens's criticism of English institutions is presented against a background of friendly, earthy and attractive English traditions. All the beer-and-stagecoach side of the early Dickens has a nostalgic, idealised solidity. The flavour of this is so strong that some readers actually suppose (as Chesterton was inclined to do) that it represents his most important achievement. I compared Dickens's criticism of England to a man barging against a locked door. One might add that Sam Weller, beer, stagecoaches, the village green, and turkey and plum pudding provide a thick plush cushion on the door which protects both the door and the assailant from serious damage.

Now it is true that this side of Dickens, the primitive, feudal, pre-industrial, became steadily weaker as time went on. The decisive appearance of the railways in *Dombey and Son* is a turning point, not only in Dickens's career, but perhaps also in the history of the novel. By the time *Our Mutual Friend* was written the cushion has worn pretty thin, but it has not completely disappeared. There is still a touch of ancient grandeur about the Thames. There is still a touch of the ancient English gentleman in Lightwood and Wrayburn, and an old-fashioned plebeian dignity in Betty Higden, surrounded and stifled though they are by Veneerings and Podsnaps. Now, of course, in the American scenes of *Martin Chuzzlewit* all this is absent. But there is absolutely nothing to take its place. A glance at the works of Hawthorne or at *The Bostonians* of Henry James will show that this was not due just to some historical lack in the real America. It was simply that the elemental John Bull in Dickens was incapable of grasping imaginatively and emotionally the strength of alien traditions, even when, as in America, those traditions had close associations with England. When he went to France and Italy his failure to understand was naturally even more complete.

The result is that the American chapters of *Martin*

Chuzzlewit, with their wild criticism show up the deep
English conservatism in Dickens, of which he was largely
unaware. His anger is much nearer to the moral and
personal anger of Samuel Johnson than to the reforming
anger of J. S. Mill. His grotesque parodies of certain
English institutions are much nearer to the generalised
poetic grotesque of Kafka than to the revolutionary criticism
of Marx. It is a strangely neglected fact that most of the
social abuses castigated by Dickens had already ceased to
exist when he wrote about them. No active reformer would
have thought this worthwhile. But a novelist may well find
the troubles of his childhood more immediate than those of
his adult years.

It may well seem that this analysis attempts to prove too
much. If the revolutionary, and even the reforming Dickens
are largely mythical, what, one may fairly ask, is the source
of the myth's abiding strength? The answer lies mainly, I
think, not in Dickens's opinions, nor in the actual political
tendencies which can be discerned in his books, but in his
hypnotic power over the reader's imagination. When
William Morris made use of Dickens for socialist propaganda, when Macaulay made his famous remark about the
sullen socialism of *Hard Times*, they were not really dis-
cerning a political creed in Dickens's work. For one thing
the word "socialism" had no agreed meaning whatever in the
England of 1860; it was for most people a word of vague
abuse directed against people whose ideas disturbed respectable opinion. Now Dickens's novels can be very disturbing,
and it was a very natural error to associate this disturbance
with imaginary political tendencies. Perhaps, indeed, we are
too severe on Macaulay in calling his comment an error, for
if the same word will properly describe Lord Attlee, William
Morris and Josef Stalin, why should it not also describe
Dickens as well? Or Queen Victoria? But the fact is that

the moral system contained in *Hard Times* cannot be trans-
lated into political terms at all. The book suggests that trade
unions are bad, but perhaps only in their operation, not in
their essence; it suggests that wanting higher wages is not
the same as wanting to dine off gold plate, and it suggests
that men like Bounderby, being selfish and dishonest in
private life, are likely to be bad employers. There is no
political creed implied here, and when he comes nearest to a
direct political statement (about trade unions) he is on the
conservative side. But when he discusses the moral theories
of Bentham, Dickens does not suggest, he delivers a
shattering attack, because he believed that it was a theory
which ignored human nature. And the human nature which
Dickens depicts as trodden underfoot by Bentham, but
inexorably reasserting itself, is the old unchanging im-
penetrable essence, manifesting itself in passion, generosity
and hatred. It has only an accidental connection with the
nineteenth century and with social questions. But though
it would be difficult to dispute this conclusion seriously,
nevertheless both William Morris and Macaulay, in their
opposite ways, were making a serious point. Dickens's
extraordinary mastery of exact observation, played upon and
transfigured by varying shades of strange imaginative light,
was bound to have a profound effect on his readers' vision
of contemporary society, and thus indirectly on their
political attitudes. Take for instance Macaulay's famous
passage about Maynooth.

> When I remember what we have taken from the Roman
> Catholics—King's College, New College, Christ Church,
> my own Trinity; and when I look at the miserable
> Dotheboys Hall which we have given them in exchange,
> I feel, I must own, less proud than I could wish of being
> a Protestant and a Cambridge man.

Now it is obvious to anyone, after a moment's thought, that the parallel between Maynooth and Dotheboys Hall is extremely remote. And Macaulay is not complaining about educational standards, for which Irish Catholics themselves would be responsible, but the paucity of the buildings and the mean scale of endowments provided by Protestant England. Maynooth was not a school, and no one was compelled to go to it. Moreover, Dickens with his John Bullish hatred of the medieval past would never have seen for himself the parallel to which Macaulay draws attention. With his Philistine attitude to the visual arts, he would never have felt any keen interest in the buildings of Cambridge. Why then does Macaulay introduce such an irrelevant comparison? For the same very good reason as toffee manufacturers like to use Micawber and Pickwick in their advertisements. Not for the sake of Dickens the reformer, but for the sake of Dickens the spellbinder, the unrivalled master of a nation's imagination. Every reader of Macaulay's passage would feel a thrill of remembered horror and anger at the mention of Dotheboys. To associate the meanness of the Government, however illogically, with the meanness of Squeers was worth pages of purple rhetoric. And such, it would seem, was the greater part of Dickens's influence on practical affairs. He brought certain issues, formerly buried in blue books and statistics into imaginative currency. However unrealistic his picture of an institution might be, its obsessive detail gave an impression of super-abundant reality. The reading of his books stimulated the growth of ideas that never entered his head.

Take, for instance, his description of Coketown in *Hard Times*.

It was a town of red brick, or of brick that would have

been red if the smoke and ashes had allowed it; but as matters stood it was a town of unnatural red and black like the painted face of a savage. It was a town of machinery and tall chimneys, out of which interminable serpents of smoke trailed themselves for ever and ever, and never got uncoiled. It had a black canal in it, and a river that ran purple with ill-smelling dye, and vast piles of building full of windows where there was a rattling and trembling all day long, and where the piston of the steam engine worked monotonously up and down like the head of an elephant in a state of melancholy madness.

The ordinary educated man of 1854, looking out upon industrial society, was aware of a confused mass of impressions and ideas. He often had no principle on which to select his data. His moral convictions could not help him to decide whether factory chimneys and smoke were, in the end, good or bad. Most of the literature with which he was familiar had little to say on the subject; *Vanity Fair*, for instance told him a lot about the merchants, but very little about the things they sold, and nothing at all about the people who made these things. Tennyson wrote about coal mines and factories in much the same style that he employed for Arthurian legend.

And then this educated man, his mind perhaps divided between abstract slogans about industrial progress and commercial greatness, and abstract, statistical denunciations of sweated labour, might read the passage I have quoted. He was being offered the means to a new vision of industrial society. It became a kind of Dantesque Inferno, full of horror, but possessing also a weird beauty, and an order imposed by the artist's eye. It could be a profound experience. It could be comparable in its force to the experience of those who first shared Wordsworth's vision of nature or

Coleridge's vision of society. But it would be stranger than these (because nature and society were already stock literary subjects, and factories were not); and as "everybody" read Dickens, the experience might be much more widely diffused.

But, of course, the ultimate consequences of an attentive reading of Wordsworth, and an attempt to share his vision are unpredictable. One might be led, as Wordsworth himself was, to religion as the ultimate ground and guarantee of the experience of nature. One might be led, as Leslie Stephen was, to the view that this vision of nature could take the place of religion. Others would share Mill's relief at no longer feeling like a calculating machine; and others again like Matthew Arnold would see in Wordsworth a complete moral system. Though Dickens was a seminal mind influencing later nineteenth-century views of the industrial revolution, the intellectual content of his vision was less than Wordsworth's, much less than Coleridge's. So perhaps even more than they, he influenced people towards many different goals, some of which he disliked, others he did not understand. The essential point of truth in the myth of Dickens the reformer lies here—in the formidable power of his imaginative influence.

II

Many of the leading political controversies of the nineteenth century turned on the question of the value or the necessity of intervention by the state. What responsibility has the state for social conditions? Dickens treated this crucial problem with his customary loud-mouthed evasiveness. The state was always wrong. If it acted, this was bureaucratic and tyrannical conduct; if it failed to act, it was lazy and incompetent. He shows us Betty Higden running away from public assistance as from an avenging fury. He shows us Jo the crossing sweeper perishing for lack of public assistance, and then preaches a fierce sermon to " lords and gentlemen, right reverends and wrong reverends of every order" who ought to have prevented his death. Dickens's version of a public department, the Circumlocution Office in *Little Dorrit*, is in some ways a brilliant portrait. It catches exactly, as perhaps no other writer has done, the ethos of a class of officials who regard their official position as secondary and dependent upon their social position, and therefore quell intruders more with social snubs than with books of rules. And Dickens hits off perfectly that subtle note of informal formality of the English upper class at work. (" You mustn't come here, saying you want to know, you know.") The pilgrimage of Clennam and Daniel Doyce through the corridors of Whitehall is splendid in its painful length. But its force is entirely imaginative. The scenes have no political content—a point easily tested by asking the simple question, " What is Dickens asking the Circumlocution Office to do? " The answer must be, " To let a public-spirited private citizen have his own way and act on his own initiative." In fact, he is preaching individualism, as he always does to public bodies. And when his thoughts turn to bad employers, he preaches state interference. There is no consistency, no plan, no theory.

Indeed, Dickens's sense of corporate life, and of our dependence on one another is curiously unbalanced. He had, of course, a great love of festivity; and social gatherings tended to release in him bouts of extravagant high spirits. He is justly famous for his power to evoke the happy social scene. As man and writer, he was born for festivity, a born master of ceremonies.

But there is a very great difference between this and a real awareness of corporate life. The idea that we are members one of another can only be imperfectly realised by festivity, because it implies that those who never meet, never know of each other's existence, have, as we say "nothing in common," are also bound together in some corporate life. And this idea, which is of course fundamental to Christianity, has also been the driving force of most revolutionary and reformist movements. Let us see what Dickens makes of it.

Take his use of the time-honoured theatrical device of the long-lost heir. He uses it repeatedly. In *Great Expectations* Estella is the daughter of the convict; in *Bleak House* Lady Dedlock has an illegitimate child, in *Barnaby Rudge* Chester is the father. All these and other examples have one thing in common. They all reveal unexpected links between people who would normally never meet. Now the point Dickens invariably makes is that these unexpected links are strong, sinister and terrifying. By means of them pride is brought low and the contents of the poisoned chalice are presented to the lips of him who prepared it. Affection generally plays little part in the connection. What would Estella have to say to the convict? What could Chester have in common with his son? This strange underground network of common roots, uniting the great and the humble is a source of horror and awe.

Closely linked with this sinisterly original use of traditional stagy melodramatic devices, is an odd, and (so far as I know) completely original use of dirt. A general griminess, of course, is one of the most obvious impressions we receive from Dickens's books. It becomes more and more obvious as his work develops. It is already in some of the London scenes of *Nicholas Nickleby*. By *Bleak House* (1852-53) it is too prominent to be ignored, and gains an added poignancy from the contrast with what are perhaps Dickens's most effective descriptions of the country—the chapters at

Chesney Wold, and on Boythorn's estate. In *Hard Times* and *Dombey and Son* there is only occasional relief, and in *Our Mutual Friend* it acquires a cardinal importance.

Now, historically, dirt is connected with industrialism, and with a new type of corporate society, in which people live physically closer to each other than ever before, but, in Dickens's opinion at least, were further apart spiritually than ever before. But dirt means disease, and the slums infect the air breathed by those who live in great mansions. In a society where classes can hardly meet or mix, except at the crises of melodramatic plots, the air at least is common. Infection is no respecter of persons. Dickens's imagination which was naturally fascinated by dirt, seized eagerly on this undeniable fact. The following is one of the most forceful of many passages that could be quoted:

> ... Tom goes to perdition head foremost in his old determined spirit. But he has his revenge. Even the winds are his messengers, and they serve him in these hours of darkness. There is not a drop of Tom's corrupted blood but propagates infection and contagion somewhere. It shall pollute, this very night, the choice stream (in which chemists on analysis would find the genuine nobility) of a Norman house, and his Grace shall not be able to say nay to the infamous alliance. There is not an atom of Tom's slime, not a cubic inch of any pestilential gas in which he lives, not one obscenity or degradation about him, not an ignorance, not a wickedness, not a brutality of his committing, but shall work its retribution, through every order of society, up to the proudest of the proud, and to the highest of the high.

There can be no doubt that the serious illness which Esther Summerson and her maid Charlie contract from the

slums had a symbolic force for Dickens. The innocent suffer
in place of the guilty. The disease, like the slums, is really
the fault of the Dedlocks and Coodles and Doodles.
It was one of Dickens's most persistently childish characteristics that for every disaster he had to find someone to
blame.

But childish though this is, thus crudely stated, it is an
idea capable of very subtle development in fiction. And in
Bleak House we are led by delicate, circumstantial stages to
the point where we can visualise the whole of society standing
confidently and perilously based on the crumbling founda-
tion of Tom-all-alone's, its religion and social welfare
poisoned by the innocent Jo who knows nothing and never
heard who made him; its government, law and social order
based only on the rotting Court of Chancery.

And so, what one might call the *negative* corporate sense
was highly developed in Dickens, and found at times memorable and profound artistic expression. But what of the
positive corporate sense? How severe he is on those who
try to do something about the abuses and miseries he complains of. How angry he is that Mrs. Jellyby should be
interested in the Africans instead of her family and the
people of London. But when he turns his attention to Mrs.
Pardiggle, who tries to do something for the people of
London, how angry he becomes with her. Take, for instance,
the speech of one of the disreputable poor who resents
Mrs. Pardiggle's visit.

How have I been conducting of myself? Why I've been
drunk for three days; and I'd a been drunk four, if I'd a
had the money. Don't I mean for to go to church? No,
I don't never mean for to go to church. I shouldn't
be expected there, if I did; the beadle's too genteel
for me. And how did my wife get that black eye?

Why I giv' it her; and if she says I didn't, she's a lie.

Is this man's resentment really all Mrs. Pardiggle's fault? Would it be so easy to placate him? or to help him? to talk to him about religion? Dickens's implied answer to all these questions is a hearty "yes." And Mr. Jarndyce is presented as the true example of wise charity and of the right use of wealth. But—and one wonders if Dickens was fully aware of this—all the poor people Mr. Jarndyce helps are humble and grateful—the sort of people it is a pleasure to help if you have the means. But the man whose speech was just quoted is not allowed by the author to receive offers of help from Jarndyce. Perhaps it is just as well.

Indeed, that speech was a portent, the importance of which Dickens did not recognise. With his wonderful ear for voices and incomparable sensitiveness to social types, he here stated with perfect clearness and brevity the basic problem of a brutalised proletariat. But if, as well as stating it, he had really grasped it intellectually, he would not have been so severe on poor Mrs. Pardiggle. Many devoted and intelligent men have given much thought to the problem of religious teaching in the slums. None of them has found it easy, and Dickens who could *see* the man who was the essence of the problem more clearly than anyone else, could only offer feeble self-satisfied solutions like this:

> Though it may be, Jo, that there is a history so interesting and affecting even to minds as near the brutes as thine, recording deeds done on this earth for common men that if the Chadbands, removing their own persons from the light, would but show it thee in simple reverence, would but leave it unimproved, would but regard it as being eloquent enough without their modest aid—it might hold thee awake, and thou might learn from it yet.

In fact, avoid being like Chadband and Mrs. Pardiggle and you'll be all right. A very jejune formula.

One could have no clearer illustration of a fundamental contrast in Dickens—the incomparable power of his imaginative observation, and the meagreness of his intellectual comment on what he had seen.

5

Crowds and Justice

It was natural for Dickens to be fascinated by crowds. He took the picaresque tradition of the lonely wanderer and endowed it with a new inward force, in *Oliver Twist* and *David Copperfield*. It was natural that while plumbing the horrors of loneliness, he should wish to consider the opposite state, in which a man is caught up in shared feelings and loses consciousness of self. Moreover, though he was himself lonely by the circumstances of his early years, and perhaps by his essential nature, he was also extremely sociable, and had a great deal of the actor's desire to merge his feelings in those of an audience. Afraid of introspection, which generally brought him pain, and at times perhaps distrustfully aware of his own aggressive instincts, he loved to forget all this in a pure surge of corporate feeling. Hence, in part, his inordinate love of giving public readings, though here, of course, we have also to reckon with his vanity. We might say that Dickens was a born leader of crowds, a man possessed with the power of transferring his feelings to an audience, and of receiving draughts of emotional strength from an audience's reaction to himself.

But in saying this, I do not mean to suggest that Dickens's recurring interest in crowds can be explained entirely by psychological factors. It is obvious enough that the image of a ruthless and triumphant mob was one of the key worries of the Victorian educated class. More perhaps than men of the twentieth century, they were inclined to take revolutions at their face value as spontaneous eruptions of popular feeling. They were haunted by the memory of the crowd which stormed the Bastille; and they found Carlyle's *French Revolution* fascinating. Dickens was seldom greatly influenced by other writers; he was at once too original and too egotistical to be a very attentive reader. One of the few literary influences which is quite unmistakable is that of Carlyle on *A Tale of Two Cities*. The crowd as the maker of revolution was something that Dickens could not evade.

The crowd was, therefore, a public obsession of his time, which was also, for psychological reasons a private obsession. But it also appealed to him as an artist. For the crowd raised in a very acute form the question of justice. His whole cast of mind predisposed him to regard the remote, professional, traditional justice of the English courts as an aristocratic sham, or what he called in *Bleak House* "wiglomeration." But to feel justified in this rather easy satirical view, he needed to examine its opposite, popular justice, based on the instincts of the crowd. In one crucial chapter of *A Tale of Two Cities*, entitled " Triumph," he strangely combines the two, and inquires what happens when the remote panoply of justice is divorced from tradition and fed with bursts of popular feeling.

His judges sat upon the bench in feathered hats; but the rough red cap and tricoloured cockade was the headdress otherwise prevailing. Looking at the Jury and the turbulent audience, he might have thought that the usual order of things was reversed, and that the felons were trying the honest men. The lowest, cruellest, and worst populace of a city, never without its quantity of low, cruel, and bad, were the directing spirits of the scene: noisily commenting, applauding, disapproving, anticipating, and precipitating the result, without a check.

[After Manette's favourable evidence, the prisoner Darnay is acquitted.] At every vote (the Jurymen voted aloud and individually), the populace set up a shout of applause. All the voices were in the prisoner's favour, and the President declared him free.

Then, began one of those extraordinary scenes with which the populace sometimes gratified their fickleness, or their better impulses towards generosity and mercy, or which they regarded as some set-off against their swollen account of cruel rage. . . . No sooner was the acquittal pronounced, than tears were shed as freely as blood at another time, and such fraternal embraces were bestowed upon the prisoner by as many of both sexes as could rush at him, that after his long and unwholesome confinement he was in danger of fainting from exhaustion; none the less, because he knew very well, that the same people, carried by another current, would have rushed at him with the very same intensity, to rend him to pieces and strew him over the streets.

These passages will give some idea of what the whole chapter shows so brilliantly—the very close connection between the positive and negative impulses of the crowd, between generosity, hero worship and lust for blood. It does not seem at all incongruous when Darnay is arrested once again, and when, as the evidence against him is read, " A terrible sound arose when the reading of this document was done. A sound of craving and eagerness that had nothing articulate in it but blood."

Perhaps Dickens was less conscious of a second similarity of opposites in this chapter. Despite the passionate and illogical nature of the justice of this court, we find a curious likeness to the deaf forgetfulness which bedevils the purely formal text book justice of *Bleak House*. Thus, " There were twenty-three names, but only twenty were responded to; for one of the prisoners so summoned had died in gaol and been forgotten, and two had already been guillotined and forgotten." The strangest thing about this odd comparison is that Dickens never really pointed to it. He was capable of seeing the evils of both systems with unequalled penetration, but not (at this stage of his life) of balancing evils against each other. It seems to be tacitly assumed in the French scenes of *A Tale of Two Cities* that fair English justice, professional judges and the rules of evidence would put things right at once. In *Bleak House* we are led to suppose that a warm empirical human type of justice would cure the ills produced by the Court of Chancery. Both assumptions might be fair, but they need to be placed together before they can be fully tested.

But if Dickens did not fully meet this need, he showed that he was aware of it in the chapter entitled "A Sight." For here we have a version of the fixed, settled, conservative barbarity of English law, which enjoins hanging and quartering. There are two reasons why this contrast is not so effective as it should be. The English scenes are so much less intense and so much briefer than the French that their impact is easily forgotten. And there is no attempt to probe the inner tragedy of the contrast. Each form of law is shown at the time as laughably and obviously wrong. Dickens makes it seem easy in either case to put things right. He does not appear to ask himself whether, by correcting one set of errors, men are not liable to glide, without realising it, into an opposite set. One part of Dickens's growth into a mature artist can be expressed thus: he gradually came to realise that it was not easy to do right.

But if his conception of justice was still a little facile when he wrote *A Tale of Two Cities*, he had already a firm grasp on the moral ambiguity of crowds. And the French scenes of mob justice stand out in splendid relief if compared with an earlier attempt in the same vein, the passage in *Oliver Twist* where the crowd yell for the death of Fagin.

The fiftieth chapter of *Oliver Twist*, memorable though it is, is, morally speaking, a failure. For it evades altogether the real problem of mob-justice. Sikes is crawling along a roof, trying to escape from the ferocious crowd. He has a rope and ties it to a chimney stack so that he can swing down to the ground on it. He accidentally hangs himself. The assumptions here are very simple. Sikes is a bad man, who deserves punishment. Therefore the crowd that howls for his death is right, therefore the crowd's feelings are really just and humane. The manner of his death is very significant. Hanging is the very same death which the law, after trying him with perfect coolness and impartiality, would have inflicted on him. That is to say, the audience are permitted to have all the satisfaction of a lynching without the material guilt of laying a finger on the man. The accident appears to provide a perfect moral loophole. But, of course, the contriver of the accident is the author; and he connives at a fake lynching which is all the more distasteful for being presented as nobody's fault. It is very like the bogus solution of the problem of the prison in *Pickwick Papers*. Once again we witness a familiar process—the young Dickens presenting his obsessions and his impulses towards violence in a crude disguise, without admitting their real nature. But this is interesting because it is a stage on the road by which he would later make these same obsessions the material of great works.

II

Both *Barnaby Rudge* and *A Tale of Two Cities* have very impressive crowd scenes, and the contrast between them is interesting. In Chapters 43 and 44 of *Barnaby Rudge* we get a glimpse of the forces that are preparing the riots. They are all accidental; it is a matter of personalities, not of social forces. Lord George, the weak visionary, and Gashford, the hypocritical mercenary, make a perfect combination for exciting the populace. Chester, with his smooth talk of his conscience being opposed to the relief of Catholics, and Dennis with his simple faith in the virtues of hanging (and the wickedness of burning) are memorable but grotesque. Powerful as psychological studies (particularly Dennis) no one could mistake them for representative figures in a great social change. The whole story suggests that crowds can be manipulated by a few individuals for a short time, but that a normal inertia and calm will soon return. " The general arrangement was, except to the few chiefs and leaders, as unintelligible as the plan of a great battle to the meanest soldier in the field." Now the leaders are essentially the familiar Dickensian eccentrics of his earliest books. True, they are presented with much greater psychological depth, and Dennis in particular possesses a deep interest. But this hardly affects the position of the crowd. The crimes of the English crowds in *Barnaby Rudge* are endowed with no serious meaning. They are only transitory acts of hooliganism, manipulated by a few gifted eccentrics. The crowd will cool off and English life will return to normal.

But in writing of the Paris mob in *A Tale of Two Cities*, Dickens took a very different line. The Paris crowd is, from the start, an irresistible social force produced by inexorable causes. Partly this reflects the deep impression which

Carlyle had made upon him. Partly it reflects his ignorance of French culture, which made it difficult for him to imagine the human variations which he saw so clearly in the apparent sameness of the London crowd. And then, we are all subject to the influence of hindsight, and no one could feel quite the same about a riot which had fizzled out, and a great revolution which had changed the world.

The influence of Carlyle was mixed. Without him Dickens, who rather lacked historical imagination might not have been stirred to write about the French Revolution at all. But Carlyle endued him with a spurious certainty about the inevitability of revolutions. There is a great deal of this kind of stuff:

> " It does not take a long time to strike a man with Lightning," said Defarge.
> " How long," demanded madame composedly, " does it take to make and store the lightning? Tell me."
> Defarge raised his head thoughtfully, as if there were something in that too.
> " It does not take a long time," said madame, " for an earthquake to swallow a town. Eh well! Tell me how long it takes to prepare the earthquake? "

There is a great deal about the blindness of those who looked at the Revolution as if it were the only harvest ever known under skies which had not been sown. And the decadent behaviour of the aristocracy in sipping their chocolate and attending to their lap-dogs brings about, as an inevitable result, the guillotine. But it would be easy to point to the equally decadent behaviour of the English aristocracy in *Barnaby Rudge* which brings no revolution.

The difference is well shown by the automatism of the French crowd. It is called "an ocean," "a raging flood," "a whirlpool of boiling waters." We are told that the men who

compose it have no personal hopes and fears; their individuality is swallowed up. Of course there is no Barnaby
in the French crowd—no one carried innocently along without interior assent. And the social satire in *Barnaby Rudge*,
though savage at times, is in the tradition of Fielding. It is
at once savage and good-humoured. It is taken for granted
that the traditional English social system is far too solidly
based to be disturbed by the brutal stupidity of some of its
officers. For instance:

> "An idiot, eh?" said the gentleman looking at
> Barnaby as he spoke. "And how long hast been an
> idiot?"
> "She knows," was Barnaby's timid answer, pointing
> to his mother. "—I—always, I believe."
> "From his birth," said the widow.
> "I don't believe it," cried the gentleman, "not a bit
> of it. It's an excuse not to work. There's nothing like
> flogging to cure that disorder."

In France words like these would be the herald of a new
social order.

III

The memorable ferocity of the crowd in *Barnaby Rudge*
(nourished by images of fire), does not drown individuality.
It is rather the other way about. Our knowledge of the
thoughts and personality of three or four people in the crowd
imperceptibly modifies our view of the crowd itself. Barnaby
himself is a bright vision: "With his flag in his hand, [he]
stood sentry in the little patch of sunlight at the distant door,
or walked to and fro outside, singing softly to himself, and
keeping time to the music of some clear church bells.
Whether he stood still, leaning with both hands on the flag-

staff, or, bearing it upon his shoulder, paced slowly up and down, the careful arrangement of his poor dress, and his erect and lofty bearing, showed how high a sense he had of the great importance of his trust, and how happy and how proud it made him. To Hugh and his companion, who lay in a dark corner of the gloomy shed, he, and the sunlight, and the peaceful Sabbath sound to which he made response, seemed like a bright picture framed by the door, and set off by the stable's blackness."

This moment of repose in the midst of scenes of violence tends to show up violence as temporary and futile. And the horror of the disciplined acts of destruction which the crowd performs is in one way relieved, and in another intensified by this and other beautiful impressions of Barnaby's separateness. His presence is a hint that all will be well. He is not the sort of character who can come to a bad end. Even when he is sentenced to death, and standing before the gallows, we can have no real anxiety for him. He is bound to be reprieved. (I leave on one side the interesting and difficult question, whether this invulnerability should be regarded as sentimental or as symbolically right.) And no crowd can impair his inner solitude. When he is arrested and placed in a lonely cell, the change in his fortunes hardly seems important, for he was just as solitary before. And here perhaps lies his main emotional value for the author— intensely and simultaneously aware of solitude and of crowds.

If other members of the crowd are not solitary, as Barnaby is, many of them are working off personal scores; and Dickens cleverly combines their personal motives with the idea of a rigid military discipline, whose ultimate purposes are obscure.

It was perfectly notorious to the assemblage that the

largest body, which comprehended about two-thirds of
the whole, was designed for the attack on Newgate. It
comprehended all the rioters who had been conspicuous
in any of their former proceedings; all those whose companions had been taken in the riots; and a great number
of people who were relatives or friends of felons in the jail.
This class included, not only the most desperate and
utterly abandoned villains in London, but some who were
comparatively innocent. There was more than one woman
there, disguised in man's attire, and bent upon the rescue
of a child or brother. There were the two sons of a man
who lay under sentence of death, and who was to be
executed along with three others on the next day but one.
There was a great party of boys whose fellow pickpockets
were in the prison; and at the skirts of all, a score of
miserable women, outcasts from the world, seeking to
release some other fallen creature as miserable as themselves, or moved by a general sympathy perhaps—God
knows—with all who were without hope and wretched.

To stress the idea of mixed motives (and perhaps in
obedience to his view of the historical facts) Dickens has
made Gordon, the supposed leader, a pawn in the hands of
the *éminence grise*, Gashford. Like Barnaby, Gordon by his
naïvety, covers the crowd scenes, furious as they are, with a
touch of romantic innocence.

But, of course, the most formidable eccentric in the crowd
is Dennis, the hangman; and he is a figure of cardinal
importance, not only in *Barnaby Rudge*, but in Dickens's
work as a whole. For he embodies the clash of ideas, that
permanently haunted his creator, the clash of law and
violence. As hangman, he is a pillar of the constitution, the
servant, as it were, of the great Lord Mansfield whose house
is gutted by the mob, and whose law books are symbolically

damaged or destroyed by their lawlessness. But he is also the fiercest member of the mob, and he is conscious of an insane logic in the contradiction.

> " I've heard the judge say, sometimes, to a highwayman or housebreaker as had tied the ladies neck and heels— you'll excuse me making mention of it, my darlings—and put 'em in a cellar, that he showed no consideration to women. Now, I say that there judge didn't know his business, brother; and that if I had been that there highwayman or housebreaker, I should have made answer: " What are you a talking of, my lord? I showed the women as much consideration as the law does, and what more would you have me do?' If you was to count up in the newspapers the number of females as have been worked off in this here city alone, in the last ten year," said Mr. Dennis thoughtfully, " you'd be surprised at the total—quite amazed, you would. There's a signified and equal thing; a beautiful thing."

In the person of Dennis, perhaps for the first time, the Dickensian eccentric comes of age. Here is an eccentric who is self-conscious, who deliberately exploits his own vagaries, and enjoys the bizarre impression he makes on others. He is able to regard his own desperate or sadistic impulses in much the same amiable spirit as Dickens himself had previously shown in presenting the absurdities of Tony Weller.

> It would have been strange enough, a man's enjoying himself in this quiet manner, while the prison was burning, and such a tumult was cleaving the air though he had been outside the walls. But here, in the very heart of the building, and moreover with the prayers of the four men under sentence sounding in his ears, and their hands,

stretched out through the gratings in their cell doors, clasped in frantic entreaty before his very eyes, it was particularly remarkable. Indeed, Mr. Dennis appeared to think it an uncommon circumstance and to banter himself upon it; for he thrust his hat on one side as some men do when they are in a waggish humour, sucked the head of his stick with a higher relish, and smiled as though he would say, " Dennis, you're a rum dog; you're a queer fellow; you're capital company, Dennis, and quite a character! "

There will, of course, be other amiable eccentrics in Dickens's work after *Barnaby Rudge*, notably in *David Copperfield*, which, as we shall see, is in some ways a reversion to an earlier type. But seldom, if ever again, shall we find an eccentric presented quite simply at his face value as he had been in *Pickwick Papers*. The hint given here of the moral depths lurking in the eccentric's attitude to himself will be taken up and developed in characters like Harold Skimpole and Joe Bagstock. And the type of character who would once have made an early Dickensian eccentric, becomes serious once he is seen in relation to society.

When Dennis invades his own sanctuary and enters the Newgate prison on the tide of mob revolution, he does not for one moment forget his proud position in society. Pointing to a man who had been shot dead, he says: " Look at this man. Do you call this constitootional? Do you see him shot through and through instead of being worked off like a Briton? Damme, if I know which party to side with. You're as bad as the other. What's to become of the country if the military power's to go a superseding the ciwilians in this way? Where's this poor fellow-creetur's rights as a citizen, that he didn't have *me* in his last moments? I was here. I was willing. I was ready. These are nice times, brother, to have the dead crying out against us in this way, and sleep comfortably in our beds arterwards; wery nice!"

Dennis is more logical than his companions realise. For the revolt is not against the government, but against a minority disliked by the government. The solemn, frightened, kindly magistrates who tell Haredale how unfortunate it is that he is a Catholic when he requires protection from the law, find in Dennis a grotesque but recognisable parody of their own conception of the constitution.

Dennis is astonished when some of his companions in the mob restrain him from performing a hanging. This also is grotesque, but serious. It makes a pertinent comment on the penalties approved by our venerable constitution. As a representative of the darker side of law and justice, and of the strange passions that lurk beneath the calm logic of just retribution for crime, Dennis has seldom been surpassed.

His whole relation to the crowd is in keeping with this dual character, the scheming, self-conscious eccentric and the living parody of legal tradition. He associates himself with rebels not because he loves rebellion, but because he loves violence. His attitude to the men in the condemned cells is sternly consistent with his permanent character as executioner, and not at all with his accidental character of rebel. He is a guardian of order. Mingling with the crowd he is untouched by mass emotions. His passions are fierce, yet congealed into an icy pattern of changeless calm. He ends, of course, on the gallows, the hangman hanged. This is more than the stock "poetic justice" and symmetry of many other Victorian plots. It is also a parable of society's attitude to the enforcement of law. Those who are most convinced that hanging is a glorious part of the constitution do not therefore respect the hangman personally. Dickens seems to mean that the hangman was a scapegoat upon whom were loaded the conscious residue of suppressed impulses of cruelty and of guilt felt on account of that cruelty. To hang the hangman is a violent but scarcely exaggerated version of this widespread set of feelings.

The description of the crowd which awaits the hangings at the end of the book strongly reinforces this idea.

" In some of the houses, people were busy taking out the window sashes for the better accommodation of spectators; in others, the spectators were already seated, and beguiling the time with cards, or drink, or jokes among themselves. Some had purchased seats upon the house tops, and were already crawling to their stations from parapet and garret window." These are ordinary law-abiding citizens and the calm, cheerful, "innocent," sadism is very like Dennis's own, though less conscious and probably less habitual than his. In showing the connection between justice and violence, Dickens here amply repaired the failure in *Oliver Twist*, where, as we have seen, he connived at the crowd's self-deception as their sadistic feelings were accidentally satisfied.

The other link between order and violence established by the plot of *Barnaby Rudge* is stagy and melodramatic, but nevertheless important. The correct and heartless eighteenth-century figure, Chester, proves to be the father of the criminal Hugh. It is true that this sort of unexpected relationship is part of the traditional machinery of the English theatre and prose romance. But Dickens's attitude to melodrama was complex. He certainly shared with the bulk of his readers a love of fantastic and violent impro-babilities; but he was also developing into a major artist capable of the subtlest effects. His symbolism provided a bridge. He could use melodramatic effects in his mature art because he was aware in his own way of the deep psychological roots of melodramatic conventions.

IV

The scenes in which the enraged crowd storm Newgate prison are very impressive; they owe something perhaps to *The Heart of Midlothian*, but the total effect is original. They contain touches of excellent psychological detail, such as the passionate fear of death by fire or violence shown by men condemned to die very soon by order of law. But their main interest lies in the first clash of two Dickensian images— crowd and prison. In the passage which follows there is a suggestion of the grappling of two obsessions, almost of irresistible force and immovable object.

> And now the strokes began to fall like hail upon the gate, and on the strong building; for those who could not reach the door, spent their fierce rage on anything—even on the great blocks of stone, which shivered their weapons into fragments, and made their hands and arms to tingle as if the walls were active in their stout resistance, and dealt them back their blows. The clash of iron ringing upon iron, mingled with the deafening tumult and sounded high above it, as the great sledge-hammers rattled on the nailed and plated door: the sparks flew off in showers; men worked in gangs, and at short intervals relieved each other that all their strength might be devoted to the work; but there stood the portal still, as grim and dark and strong as ever, and saving for the dints upon its battered surface, quite unchanged.

There is an unusually strong undercurrent of excitement in these chapters, and we hardly need the external evidence of a letter to Forster to guess what a deep experience the writing of them made for the author. (He wrote: " I have just burnt into Newgate, and am going for the next number to tear those prisoners out by the hair of their heads.")

These are great scenes, but it is not surprising, given Dickens's comparative immaturity at the time, and the degree to which his personal emotions were involved, that the end of *Barnaby Rudge* should be unsatisfactory. His deepest meditations on the prison would come many years later in *Little Dorrit*, while he would develop an interest in a different, more civilised type of crowd. In *Barnaby Rudge* there is a mighty clash, but no tragedy and no reconciliation.

It would be pleasant and convenient in this study where the main stress falls on Dickens's development, to point to a later work where this clash of great ideas led up to a satisfying climax and resolution. But no writer's career, certainly not the career of Dickens, is as neat and regular as critics are inclined to wish. In some ways, the crowd of *Barnaby Rudge* remains the most memorable that Dickens ever described. Yet there were developments, even if they were not all necessarily improvements. In *A Tale of Two Cities*, he contrived to give a keener impression of an invisible crowd, of mounting communal passions nursed in secret which must one day overthrow the government. Dickens had little of importance to say about the meaning of political revolution. But he was able, especially by the use of images of darkness, to convey a fine glimpse of slowly nurtured social forces coming to catastrophic fruition.

> Darkness closed around, and then came the ringing of the church bells and the distant beating of the military drums in the Palace Court-Yard, as the women sat knitting, knitting. Darkness encompassed them. Another darkness was closing in as surely, when the church bells, then ringing pleasantly in many an airy steeple over France, should be melted into thundering cannon. . . . So much

was closing in about the women who sat knitting, knitting, that they their very selves were closing in around a structure yet unbuilt, where they were to sit knitting, knitting, counting dropping heads.

Dickens never repeated these vast spectacular crowd scenes. His mind turned to different versions of the crowd. In *Little Dorrit* and *Our Mutual Friend*, the crowds are only a background, the cheerful sufferers of Bleeding Heart Yard, the swarming inhabitants of those sad streets where Arthur Clennam walks on Sundays, and remembers the miseries of his youth.

The crowd and the solitary—there is nothing really surprising in the fact that the same man should concentrate on both. The friendless solitary feels as if the whole of society were an implacable crowd. And the dual preoccupation reminds us of what was missing in Dickens. He did not understand, or at any rate, did not effectively portray family relationships. Like every novelist, of course, he described many families; but did he ever give us a convincing portrait of a marriage? On the subject of the parent-child relationship he is more lucid, but still apt to be perverse. He tends to reverse the roles. Little Dorrit is a mother to her father, not a daughter. The doll's dressmaker in *Our Mutual Friend* is a stern and terrifying stepmother to her father. Even friendship tends to develop into an unreal jollity.

Now, of course, Dickens is, or was once, a great author for family reading. And he was revered in his time, and has sometimes been attacked since, as a fanatical celebrator of the family affections. But this is deceptive. The Dickens family is not the fundamental Christian and Freudian family of father, mother and children. It is a covey of aunts, and cousins and relatives by marriage. His favourite family celebration is Christmas. That is, in England, just when the basic Christian and Freudian family is least itself, when it is a confused jumble of three or four generations, in fact, when it becomes a *crowd*.

So it is that the idea of the crowd (and the corresponding idea of the solitary) are fundamental for Dickens. They are the key to his unrivalled strength as a portrayer of industrial society, the home of crowds. They are the source of his weakness in presenting deep personal relationships. And since the deepest human affections, if denied proper expression, will become muddled and distorted, his sentimentality also can be referred to the same source.

6

Fruitful Failures

Dr. Strong's was an excellent school; as different from Mr. Creakles's as good is from evil. It was gravely and decorously ordered, and on a sound system; with an appeal, in everything, to the honour and good faith of the boys, and an avowed intention to rely on their possession of those qualities unless they proved themselves unworthy of it, which worked wonders. We all felt that we had a part in the management of the place, and in sustaining its character and dignity. Hence, we soon became warmly attached to it—I am sure I did for one, and I never knew in all my time, of any other boy being otherwise—and learnt with a good will, desiring to do it credit.

This passage from Chapter 16 of *David Copperfield* is typical of many. I suppose every careful reader of Dickens learns to recognise and dread this Dickens voice. For we soon realise that it only occurs when his imagination is not working, or when he is trying to evade an awkward idea, or when he is turning aside from his story to convince us of the purity of his sentiments. And we notice these passages the more because they contrast so strongly with his normal love of detail.

It was both the strength and the weakness of Dickens's

mind that whenever his mind was really working, he imagined with immense detail. It has already been pointed out that we know more about Mrs. Harris, who does not even exist, than about some of the leading characters of other novelists. Dickens had a very strong tendency to reduce everything to the physical. He lingers more lovingly than anyone else on food and drink, not for their own sake—he had none of the instincts of the gourmet—but as the outward sign of friendship and generosity. The physical reality of his presentation of London has never been equalled. He even feels obliged (with gross improbability) to externalise the moral triumph of Pickwick and Oliver Twist over their enemies by describing a successful physical combat.

Like some of his other idiosyncrasies, this one was so firmly rooted that he could even, occasionally, parody it. Just as the magnificent staginess of Crummles parodies the serious but absurd melodrama of the plot of *Nicholas Nickleby*, so does a passage like the following make fun of something very Dickensian:

> " Her grief," replied Traddles, with a serious look. " Her feelings generally. As I mentioned on a former occasion, she is a very superior woman, but has lost the use of her limbs. Whatever occurs to harass her, usually settles in her legs; but on this occasion it mounted to the chest, and then to the head, and, in short, pervaded the whole system in a most alarming manner."

I have said that this reduction to the concrete was both a strength and a weakness. It contributes to the extraordinary air of personal reality possessed even by psychologically absurd characters like Ralph Nickleby. It is linked with his wonderful grasp of detail in his social work, in his duties as an editor, and indeed, in all his activities. But it is linked also with his insensitiveness to ideas, and his extraordinary insistence on the factual accuracy of some of his wildest imaginings. (The preface to *Bleak House*, in which he discusses "spontaneous combustion" is a notable example.)

But since we so often have reason to be astonished at his power of evoking physical reality and his mastery of telling detail, vague abstract passages like the one first quoted stand out all the more. We find that such passages always evade the consequences of what they state. To take an obvious example; what happened if a boy in the school tried to take advantage of Dr. Strong's credulity and absentmindedness? Lacking as he was in self-criticism and self-knowledge, Dickens's evasions are often as large and obvious as this.

Another Dickens voice we learn to dread is the genteel-facetious, for instance, this chapter heading from *Nicholas Nickleby*: " Having the misfortune to deal with none but common people, is necessarily of a mean and vulgar character." The psychological sources of this tone may be very complex; Dickens had a kind of "distressed gentlefolk" sensitiveness about his own class position, and a fear of making himself common—a fear partly neutralised, but not destroyed, by his radical principles and his deeply ingrained attraction to the sordid and the violent. Then even at this early stage of his life, when he was winning easy popularity with works of mixed value, he no doubt possessed an instinctive awareness of his proper status as an artist, and could not therefore be wholly satisfied with the creaking traditional machinery of the picaresque novel. But whatever the causes, the results are clear. Reading a heading such as this, we prepare ourselves for a chapter of heavy facetiousness, where the feelings expressed are a conventional comic ideogram, infinitely remote from real human beings.

The most essential and the most obvious point about this type of writing is that the author is uneasy. It is therefore equally remote from his exuberant fantastic early humour, and his accurate and intelligent later satirical style which developed out of this early humour. Dickens's humour and satire, at its worst, as in much of *Nicholas Nickleby*, hovers between two dreary poles. One is reached when he feebly attacks the contempt for common things which nevertheless forms an undercurrent of his own writing, and the other when the objects of satire are only factitious bogies, denied human status and moral choice.

Given Dickens's impulsive temperament, and the memory of acute humiliations in his childhood and adolescence, failings such as these are not surprising. Instead of blaming them too much, we should recognise the greatness of the man who could eventually rise so far above his personal feelings as to portray with humane subtlety Dorrit in his poverty and wealth or Bounderby's mythically cruel upbringing.

Dickens was gifted, of course, with great, natural, effortless talent for writing. In tracing his arduous progress to great art, we should not ignore this obvious fact. *Pickwick Papers* may be inferior in many ways, but it is unique and deserves to remain the favourite it has always been. Nevertheless, it is fascinating to observe how slowly, and sometimes how uneasily, Dickens approached topics which provided him with some of his greatest achievements. If it is true that Dickens remains to this day unsurpassed as a novelist of industrial society, he approached the subject, in his early writing years, with hesitation. Henry James himself could not erect a more delicate façade of civilised evasion about the real sources of the wealth of the retired business man, Pickwick, the work he did and the personal qualities that led to his success. Pickwick is only, of course, in fact, a very old stock character, the benevolent squire, dressed up as a modern industrial man. The unreality of the Cheeryble brothers is even more striking because they are active in business, and we are privileged to watch them at work. Their function seems to be to exorcise (most unconvincingly), the terrors of the crude and virile industrialism of the 1830s. They represent business without balance sheets, without labour troubles, without competition, without anxiety, and therefore without any protective toughness. The evasion is obvious, and must soon have become obvious to Dickens himself. The Cheerybles are an early monument to his uneasiness about industrial society—but this same uneasiness was the material from which would come his masterly treatment of it in *Hard Times*. Hindsight enables us to say that the sentimental evasion of the Cheerybles was really a good sign. Nearly all Dickens's greatest achievements sprang from his uneasiness. He is the great poet of the things he at first most feared and falsified—money, prisons, crowds and factories.

A year or two after *Nicholas Nickleby*, when *The Old Curiosity Shop* was published, his unwillingness (or inability), to face industrial society squarely remained, but had taken a subtler form. *The Old Curiosity Shop* is not a distinguished novel, but even if it were not a milestone in the development of a great artist, it would still be fascinating as a document. Much of the book's deliberate plan is a failure. At this stage the deeper feelings of mankind only brought out the worst in Dickens, made him melodramatic and imitative. What remains interesting is the relation between town and country, and between industrial and agricultural society.

Most readers have probably felt that there was something wrong with the presentation of country scenes, but it is difficult to illustrate the trouble by quotation. Perhaps the following passage will give some idea.

" When they rose up from the ground, and took the shady track which led them through the wood, she bounded on before, printing her tiny footsteps in the moss, which rose elastic from so light a pressure and gave it back as mirrors throw off breath; and thus she lured the old man on, with many a wayward look and merry beck—now pointing stealthily to some lone bird as it perched and twittered on a branch that strayed across their path, now stopping to listen to the songs that broke the happy silence, or watch the sun as it trembled through the leaves, and, stealing in among the ivied trunks of stout old trees, opened long paths of light." The whole manner of the country passages is similar—a kind of diseased, unconvinced and unconvincing pastoral. It is a pastoral where no one really works on the land or looks after sheep. It is the bookish townsman's country, but this is never admitted. It is characteristic that no attempt is made to consider how Nell and her grandfather would enjoy sleeping in the open air. The economic life of the villagers is forgotten; and instead, with a grand, unconscious self-destructive appropriateness, we have—Mrs. Jarley's wax-works. This unconscious self-criticism occurs also in the case of Crummles in *Nicholas Nickleby*. Though not (probably) deliberate, it shows a developing critical and satirical mind at work beneath the conscious mind; Dickens was always wiser than his plans and theories.

The countryside here, then, is a place of escape. Escape from what? According to the plot, they are escaping from the dingy city and the machinations of enemies. In another sense, they seem to be escaping from logic and reality. As long as they are in the country, their normal needs and difficulties disappear. It is as if they were going backwards in time. The village church is hardly a symbol of religion; it rather represents a past period ("Gothic" and therefore romantic and fairy-like), where their troubles and respon-sibilities cannot reach them. Such an interpretation is con-firmed by the passage at the end of Chapter 43, as the wanderers approach the Black Country. They see smoke from furnaces, "tall chimneys vomiting forth a black vapour" and then, " The child and her grandfather . . . passed through a dirty lane into a crowded street, and stood, amid its din and tumult, and in the pouring rain, as strange, bewildered, and confused as if they had lived a thousand years before, and were raised from the dead and placed there by a miracle."

There follows a glimpse of a crowd of industrial workers:

In a large and lofty building, supported by pillars of iron, with great black apertures in the upper walls, open to the external air—echoing to the roof with the beating of hammers and roar of furnaces, mingled with the hissing of red-hot metal plunged in water, and a hundred strange unearthly noises never heard elsewhere—in this gloomy place, moving like demons among the flame and smoke, dimly and fitfully seen, flushed and tormented by the burning fires, and wielding great weapons, a faulty blow from any one of which must have crushed some workman's skull, a number of men laboured like giants. Others, reposing upon heaps of coal or ashes, with their faces turned to the black vault above, slept or rested from their toil. Others again, opening the white-hot furnace doors, cast fuel on the flames, which came rushing and roaring forth to meet it, and licked it up like oil. Others drew forth, with clashing noise, upon the ground, great sheets of glowing steel, emitting an insupportable heat, and a dull deep light like that which reddens in the eyes of savages.

To some extent the curious tone of this passage and of the whole of Chapter 44 can be explained as representing Nell's childish vision. But the childish vision was partly shared by the author. There is nothing in the book to modify or correct it. Industrial society is strictly localised; it is something you come to, and then rapidly pass through and escape; it is violent, terrifying, inhuman. It is a nightmare which you will soon forget when the night ends. The contrast with *Hard Times* and *Dombey and Son* is immense, and yet— Dickens was already capable of a *vision* of industrial society, even if he was hazy about its meaning and unable to connect it with other forms of life. There is a germ of future achievement in this lurid quotation. But it was not till *Dombey and Son* began to appear in 1846 that he showed his awareness that England was becoming an industrial society.

Martin Chuzzlewit, which came between *The Old Curiosity Shop* and *Dombey and Son*, gives no warning of the change. There were many centres of resistance in Dickens's mind to the change from the coaching days of *Pickwick Papers* and *Nicholas Nickleby*. There were nostalgic connections with Rochester and the old world of the English country town. There was the fear (particularly important for a man whose family was both "gentlemanly" in a rather upstart way, and financially disgraced) that business was low. There was the idea, which was bound to strike forcibly upon the mind of a born popular entertainer, that the public had a strong resistance to the literary examination of recent social changes. The popularity of Scott, the more recent success of Bulwer Lytton and the "silver-spoon" novelists were alike a solemn warning. Then there were great technical difficulties. To deal faithfully with industrial society, it is necessary to convey the sense of a crowd all working in one direction, yet containing a variety of personal hopes and fears. Scott could help him here, and he showed in *Barnaby Rudge* that he learnt something from the masterly handling of the crowd in *The Heart of Midlothian*.

Though *Barnaby Rudge* is set in the eighteenth century, and contains no industrial scenes, it still has an important place in the development of Dickens as the poet of industrial society.

However, at the time of writing *The Old Curiosity Shop*, Dickens had neither the emotional nor the technical equipment for these intractable subjects, and one can hear the author's sigh of relief as the travellers emerge into the country again. But these chapters provide a good illustration of an important general point. His minor works, and even his failures gain immensely from being seen as part of his whole development. He was a slow learner, and at times his mental processes almost seem to resemble the unseen and inexorable formation of geological strata. He often did not know himself what was going on beneath the surface; but when the changes were complete they brought a satisfying rock-like strength.

II

Dickens possessed from the first a deeply-felt respect for the primary human impulses. In the *Pickwick Papers* era, this led him to a superficial assurance that if you do as you like, all will be well. It was linked, at this stage, with his easy acceptance of fantasy, and disregard of the logic of events. But his optimism soon developed into a serious criticism of the fashionable "progressive" doctrines derived from Bentham and Macaulay. Even in *The Old Curiosity Shop* we have this hit at Macaulay's set: "Don't you feel how naughty it is of you to be a waxwork child, when you might have the proud consciousness of assisting, to the extent of your infant powers, the manufacturers of your country; of improving your mind by the constant contemplation of the steam engine?" The waxworks may be absurd, but they are already fulfilling part of the function that the circus-riders have in *Hard Times*; and the humane developed criticism of utilitarianism given by the later book is already foreshadowed.

All this was conscious and deliberate. But, like most people, though in a much higher degree than most, Dickens was fascinated by violence. The evasive and inchoate form in which it appears here goes far to ruin the book. Dickens has recorded in the *Uncommercial Traveller* the perennial sway exercised over his mind by the story of Captain Murderer. Captain Murderer married a series of wives, instructed them to make pastry for a huge pie, and then after killing them ate the pies with the women's flesh as meat. This went on until one woman learnt what was happening, consumed a slow but deadly poison, and thus caused the death of the captain when he ate a pie containing her flesh. Dickens could not, of course, exclude from his work the morbidity of temperament which was so deeply stirred by stories like this. But in his early works it is present without any artistic assimilation. It is present, for instance, in the Gothic tales of horror carelessly scattered through *Pickwick Papers*, in unfunny jokes about such things as sausage machines containing the wrong material, and in the pharisaical gusto with which he describes the senile raptures of Gride in *Nicholas Nickleby*. It is present, above all, in Quilp's sadism. It is noticeable that Quilp is not content with ordinary violence and terrorism. His imagination runs on more exquisite torture: " I'll beat you with an iron rod, I'll scratch you with a rusty nail, I'll pinch your eyes if you talk to me." And his cruelty is (not very obtrusively) linked in true sadistic fashion with sexual morbidity. " Ah, what a nice kiss that was—just upon the rosy part! What a capital kiss." This is a mild example, but still significant in view of the limits set by conventional agreement upon an open discussion of such things. And these sadistic thrills of Quilp are matched by the horrified nightmares of Oliver Twist, or of Nell herself, when, for instance, she thinks: " If he were to die—if sudden illness had happened to him, and he were never to come home again alive—if, one night, he should come home, and kiss and bless her as usual, and after she had gone to bed and had fallen asleep, and was perhaps dreaming pleasantly, and smiling in her sleep, he should kill himself, and his blood come creeping, creeping on the ground to her own bedroom door." It is an old platitude to call the death of Little Nell the most sentimental scene that Dickens ever wrote; and it is a platitude which contains truth. Sentimentality is a difficult word to define. I use it here to mean a falsification caused by an honest, because unconscious, evasion of some fact, desire or fear, which is too shocking to be faced. From this point of view it is not surprising that the death of Little Nell should provide a classic example. Dickens's morbid temperament would naturally feast upon a little girl's suffering, while his moral sense told him he should feel only pity and grief. (Of course I am not blaming his moral sense for the badness of the passage. For it is easy to see that the description of Little Nell's death, bad as it is, would be very much worse, if the suppressed morbid enjoyment had been given free rein.) His religious attitude, emotional but lacking a firm intellectual basis, made him uneasy and overemphatic on the subject of death. On this point the excellent summary of the late Humphry House cannot be improved upon:

" Their popularity (i.e. popularity of such scenes) at the time is partly explained by the fact that a religion in a state of transition from supernatural belief to humanism is very poorly equipped to face death, and must dwell on it for that very reason."

Finally, there is a curious kind of sexual attraction in the sexlessness of the prematurely-wise female child, which was a strong influence on several leading Victorians. So Little Nell in death combines in herself several of the things which made Dickens most uneasy, death and religion, female purity, and cruelty to the weak. It is no wonder the passage is a byword for sentimentality. But even there was the seed of something valuable: and *Little Dorrit* largely succeeds where *The Old Curiosity Shop* fails in presenting the child on whom responsibility is forced.

Throughout these early works morbid feelings are satisfied without being admitted. They are not brought into relation with normal human impulses. Instead, they are laughed off as meaningless jokes, or relegated to some impossible region of literary Gothic horror, or, in the case of Quilp and Gride, they are externalised in people who have no share of our common humanity, who excite no sympathy, encourage no reader to self-questionings. Quilp's sadism, Gride's drivelling enjoyment of youth and beauty are the unchanging, unexplained qualities of ogres. They are beyond criticism and analysis. Their moral deformity, like the physical deformity of the one, and the disgusting senility of the other, are only fairytale obstacles which the princess and the knight errant must avoid. They may provide an enjoyable thrill of horror or a cheap glow of indignation, but for the reader who is not carried away by these easy emotions, they largely cease to function at all and become absurd. In making this facile use of deep and dangerous impulses, Dickens was, of course, assisted by the tradition of English stage melodrama.

Chesterton, a penetrating though one-sided critic of Dickens, once said that the serious part of Dickens's work was his comedy. As a general statement this cannot stand; it cannot be made to fit *Little Dorrit* or *Great Expectations*. But applied to some of the early works, and particularly to *Nicholas Nickleby*, it contains a great deal of truth. The best of *Nicholas Nickleby* deals with Crummles and the theatre. It is extremely funny, and it also contains a subtle implied criticism of the externalisation of morbid impulses, and the melodramatic treatment of evil as a mere physical obstacle to the fulfilment of one's desires. There is a fine contrast between the mean and corroding jealousies and disloyalties of the theatrical troupe, and the stagy, hilarious language in which their profession has taught them to express such feelings. From these scenes alone we might guess that Dickens would one day find a way to make use of unassimilated morbidity in the interests of his art. The comedy of Crummles prepares the way for the tragic intensity of *Our Mutual Friend* and *Great Expectations*.

7

Dombey and Son

Dombey and Son is perhaps the first important English novel that deals with industrial society. New social facts take a long time to work down to those imaginative depths where artistic creation originates, and then to work their way back upwards into a finished artistic product. (A glance at the range of novels published since 1945 will confirm this point.) *Dombey and Son* is unusual among Dickens's works, and still more unusual among the novels of the time in possessing the atmosphere of the decade in which it was written—the forties, the age of railway fever.

It entirely lacks that characteristic Dickensian backward glance, which we find romantic and preposterous in *Pickwick Papers*, blurred and nostalgic in *David Copperfield*, brooding and bitter in *Little Dorrit*. Sadness it has; but it is the sadness of the work-a-day world, caused by bereavement or loneliness or unrequited affection. There are no coaches, no eighteenth-century country scenes, no village churches. It is a London book, about a new brisk, commercial and fashionable London, where the quaint alleys and strange old inns of the earlier Dickens have disappeared or have been forgotten. It is a London which is the banking and trading centre of the world—and also, which will prove important, a great seaport. When the characters leave London, they do not enter a pastoral world, as in *Oliver Twist*, or go to quiet villages like Little Nell. They go where smart people of the forties often did go, to the vulgar, bracing atmosphere of Brighton.

The railways were an apparent sign of deep changes. Their speed, their mechanical accuracy, their remorseless "progressive" movement, all give Dickens just what he required to convey his sense of a new world. But it takes a very great artist to make much of really obvious symbols. Zola, as it seems to me, failed in *Le Bête Humaine*. Apart from a chapter or two in *Anna Karenina*, it is hard to think of a parallel book which turns railways into art.

II

Dickens wastes no time in presenting to us the leading paradoxes of industrial society. First we are shown Dombey and son together, the embodiment of the firm, the emblem of business continuity. But the son is a helpless infant. The name of the firm, which is an epitome of commercial solidity, is based on a pious wish, not on a fact. Then, in the next chapter, after Mrs. Dombey's death, the family of Dombey and the family of Toodle face each other. Toodle is a railway worker, a stoker. The link between Toodle and Dombey is the link between capital and labour. Dombey is hardly aware of any connection; but he is forced to permit a practical connection because his child must be fed after his wife's death. And so Toodle's wife Polly, is engaged to feed him. Here as so often in Dickens's mature works a perfect symbolic appropriateness goes hand-in-hand with perfect precision of detail. The whole story of the wet-nurse is credible, and the whole Toodle family is convincing. But as the milk flows from the engine driver's wife to the capitalist's child, we are aware of money and power, generally, flowing in a similar direction.

Dombey says: " It is not at all in this bargain that you need become attached to my child, or that my child become attached to you. I don't expect or desire anything of the kind. Quite the reverse. When you go away from here, you will have concluded what is a mere matter of bargain and sale, hiring and letting: and you will stay away. The child will cease to remember you; and you will cease, if you please, to remember the child." This is a more monstrous and startling version of the "normal" relations of capital and labour under the advanced liberal principles of political economy, which Dickens later analysed more thoroughly in *Hard Times*. The point is driven home by the physical contrast between Dombey and Toodle, which utterly disguises the fact that they are both complementary parts of the same industrial civilisation. One is " Strong, loose, round-shouldered, shuffling, shaggy"; "the other is one of those close-shaved, close-cut moneyed gentlemen who are glossy and crisp like new bank notes."

Dombey, of course, resents the inevitable closeness of the connection between wet-nurse and child; and later on when young Paul is dead, there is a fine economical passage illustrating this: Toodle is wearing a sign of mourning in his cap.

> His (Dombey's) attention was arrested by something in connection with the cap still going slowly round and round in the man's hand.
>
> " We lost one babby," observed Toodle, " there's no denying."
>
> " Lately," added Mr. Dombey, looking at the cap.
>
> " No, sir, up'ard of three years ago . . ."

Dombey's " Lately " is an accusation. It means " You dare

exhibit signs of grief for *my* dead son." Dombey's pride and shuddering dislike of human contacts is composed of strangely-mingled elements. Off-hand one might be tempted to call it aristocratic. But, of course, Dombey is not an aristocrat but a merchant. And this may recall to mind the odd fact that there are virtually no aristocrats in *Dombey and Son*. Major Bagstock makes a few boastful references to royalty; but apart from these there is almost no mention of anyone higher in the social scale than Dombey himself. Dickens admittedly did not excel in studies of artistocratic society, but all his books from *Nicholas Nickleby* to *Our Mutual Friend* contain aristocratic characters, except where, as in ·*Oliver Twist* the plot makes them obviously inappropriate. To deal at length with wealth and power, as he does here, and to omit the aristocracy, is odd. On the narrowly technical side, it shows Dickens's rigid adherence to his plan for making Dombey believe himself the absolute king of his own universe until the crash comes. For Victorian aristocratic contempt for trade was so well developed, that even Dombey could hardly have been immune. But it is more important to notice that Dombey lives by a parasitic pseudo-aristocratic code. His wealth and his commercial success are hereditary. They have come to him just as landed property comes to an aristocrat. And so he develops qualities which can be fatal to success in business; he is touchy, arrogant, unrealistic, unapproachable, and is a poor judge of character. When told by his sister that if there are three words in the English language which Miss Tox venerates, those words are " Dombey and Son," he replies, " Well, I believe it. It does Miss Tox credit." Such language is suited to Sir Leicester Dedlock; it is no way for a realistic business magnate to talk. From one point of view Dombey is a fascinating study of the consequences that follow when a business man apes the code of an aristocrat; the collapse of

Dombey's business, however convenient and contrived it may appear, cannot be called improbable.

As was his custom, Dickens followed out this fruitful idea into several delicate variations. Thus, Miss Pipchin, who is essentially that familiar character, "the gentlewoman who has seen better days," is not, after the usual manner, the impecunious relict of an unfortunate member of a cadet branch of a noble family. She is the widow of a business man who was ruined over the Peruvian mines. That is to say, the bogus niceties of fallen aristocratic pride are being resuscitated and reshaped in terms of the grand commercial failure. At moments like this Dickens ranks as a social historian gifted with prophetic insight.

III

Dombey's pseudo-aristocratic remoteness and carelessness of consequences give Carker his chance. As a social type, Carker, too, is prophetic. He is classless, anonymous; he has the habits of a gentleman, but they are consciously assumed, and can be dropped at will. He manipulates Dombey with a cunning mixture of servility and arrogance. He knows just how flattering a touch of mock insolence can be to a man who has always had his own way. He says, for instance, " Catch you forgetting anything. If Mr. Paul inherits your memory, he'll be a troublesome customer . . ." And the following description perfectly reflects his method; " He seemed a man who would contend against the power that vanquished him, if he could, but who was utterly borne down by the greatness and superiority of Mr. Dombey."

Neither Dombey nor Carker can direct or even understand the development of the railways. They are pictured as gradually undermining a whole way of life: " Houses were knocked down; streets broken through and stopped; deep

pits and trenches dug in the ground; enormous heaps of
earth and clay thrown up; buildings that were undermined
and shaking, propped by great beams of wood. Here, a
chaos of carts, overthrown and jumbled together, lay topsy-
turvy at the bottom of a steep unnatural hill; there, confused
treasures of iron soaked and rusted in something that had
accidentally become a pond. Everywhere were bridges that
led nowhere; thoroughfares that were wholly impassable;
Babel towers of chimneys, wanting half their height; temporary wooden houses and enclosures in the most unlikely
situations; carcasses of ragged tenements, and fragments of
unfinished walls and arches, and piles of scaffolding, and
wildernesses of bricks, and giant forms of cranes, and tripods
straddling above nothing. . . . Hot springs and fiery eruptions,
the usual attendants upon earthquakes, lent their contribu-
tions of confusion to the scene. Boiling water hissed and
heaved within dilapidated walls; whence, also, the glare and
roar of flames came issuing forth; and mounds of ashes
blocked up rights of way, and wholly changed the law and
custom of the neighbourhood."

Images of impending social change are cunningly mixed
here with the dreary immobility of the site itself. Iron rusts,
and wood is needed to provide support. The mechanical
product still needs the help of the ancient product of the
forests. The revolution is real, but incomplete; and it has
its own decay. Dickens could not always maintain the sure
touch of this passage. It is hard to take seriously the well-
known passage which begins: " Away, with a shriek, and
a roar, and a rattle . . . " (cap 20). And even the account of
Carker's death, impressive in its way, is bound to seem too
convenient. It would seem that two scarcely compatible
ideas are mingled in this famous scene. One is that railways,
or machines generally, develop an independent robot life,
which is eventually too strong for human beings, and liable

to destroy them. This is, of course, a point of the highest importance, though it is doubtful whether it is best conveyed by the sudden, melodramatic death, which may leave the reader too breathless to ponder social implications. The other idea, much more obviously suggested by Carker's death is that the train is an instrument of divine justice, used to punish the man who tried to seduce Edith Dombey. Not only is this idea hard to reconcile with the other, it is also extremely hard to realise imaginatively. It would need a much stronger and more pervasive sense of Divine Providence than Dickens could rise to, to convince us of the artistic rightness of this semi-miraculous intervention. We must, regretfully, chalk up a failure against this exciting chapter, and, as we shall see, it is part of a larger failure to imagine the real relation between Dombey and Edith.

But a few lapses do not detract from Dickens's achievement in making railways represent adequately the complexities of a new industrial order. And what is especially new in his work is the balance. Thus he follows his account of the confusion and change brought by railways, with a scene conveying a new continuity and tradition. Few writers have shown so well the speed with which people come to regard the revolutionary as itself traditional.

" There was even railway time observed in clocks, as if the sun itself had given in. Among the vanquished was the master chimney-sweeper, whilom incredulous at Staggs's Gardens, who now lived in a stuccoed house three stories high, and gave himself out, with golden flourishes upon a varnished board, as contractor for the cleansing of railway chimneys by machinery." Habit can absorb any surprise; it is one of the book's key points.

IV

Two subordinate topics fill out the picture of commercial society, relatively new, and yet already grown venerable and traditionalist. They are imperialism and prostitution. The first is no more than a reminiscent and yet violent echo issuing from Major Bagstock. With his bluff military friendliness, his crafty selfishness, and his violence against "the natives" in the person of his servant, he is a truly terrifying shadow cast across the Empire's future. And it is no credit to our penetration, but merely due to the accident of time, if we see more in him than Dickens's first readers did. The point to notice is that in the scenes between Dombey and Bagstock, each becomes representative of a whole class and way of life; and their strange friendship, based on a union of opposite characters is an emblem of a curious alliance between commercial, practical men and fire-eating militarists.

In a character like Bagstock we can see the new use to which Dickens's humorous gifts were now being put. In many ways Bagstock is a perfect example of the early Dickens character. Like Mrs. Gamp he has his own memorable style of speech, his own delectable physical and mental idiosyncrasies, his own precious absurdity. But his function is utterly changed. He is self-conscious; he manipulates his own eccentricity for profit. He is related to society, and his position as an apparent equal of Dombey, yet really his parasite, is exactly charted. He offers, as we have seen, a version of imperialism. He is a real moral being who can be judged and understood. He is still funny, but not with that irresistible self-dependent humour of Mrs. Gamp. The comic eccentric is seen in the round against the background of a whole society.

In imperialism we have a topic of great importance brilliantly handled and yet claiming only a minor part in the book's organisation. In prostitution we have an important topic treated at greater length, but with much less skill. The chief idea that Dickens brought to his treatment of the theme was simple, and one that might, with tactful handling, have yielded excellent results. It was this: in a society where buying and selling become the main activity, buying and selling will not ultimately stop short of bodies and souls. Historically, the idea has its weaknesses. (Some enthusiasts of anti-Victorian polemic write as if prostitution, instead of being the oldest trade in the world, had been invented by the capitalist nineteenth century.) Nevertheless, the idea possesses a clear moral symmetry, and a simplicity of outline capable of releasing considerable artistic power.

An elaborate parallel is constructed between Mrs. Skewton and her daughter (who marries Dombey) on the one hand, and Mrs. Brown and her daughter Alice, who has been seduced by Carker and becomes a prostitute. The comparison is made very obvious by such devices as giving Chapter 34 the heading " Another mother and daughter." One girl is "sold" to Dombey, another to Carker. Carker attempts the seduction of Edith as he has already achieved the seduction of Alice. But much of the force of the parallel is lost because the characters are so very much aware of it at the time. Edith sees the similarity even before her marriage, which would require exceptional qualities of detachment and self-analysis. And Dickens is unable to persuade us that Edith possesses them. He is guilty here of a failing very common in novelists of strong convictions—he is making a character do the author's work for him by commenting (as if from above) upon her own personality. When Mrs. Brown makes the comparison even more explicit, it is less credible still. But the parallel breaks down in the end, when

Edith, after running away from Dombey unexpectedly refuses to become Carker's mistress. It would be interesting to know why.

In any case, there are reasons why we should not expect Dickens to succeed here. It seems probable that he suffered from guilt about his unstable sexual temperament, and his failure to find lasting satisfaction in his wife. We cannot tell how forcibly he was struck by the contrast between his own conduct and his popular position as the great upholder of family life. But it seems likely that this contrast was partly responsible for his tendency to take his eye off the ball, and relapse into melodramatic evasions when writing about sexual guilt. And I should judge this factor to be at least as important as the one usually proposed; the conventional demands of Victorian prudery. Several of Dickens's contemporaries, notably George Eliot and Trollope, were able to bring a much firmer and calmer mind to bear upon the moral aspects of illicit sexual desires. Dickens was no hypocrite, but neither was he a man who understood himself. When he was worried, he became lofty and sentimental.

One significant detail will perhaps give point to these rather theoretical comments. In Mrs. Brown's home: " There was no light in the room save that which the fire afforded. Glaring sullenly from time to time like the eye of a fierce beast half asleep, it revealed no objects that needed to be jealous of a better display. A heap of rags, a heap of bones, a wretched bed, two or three mutilated chairs or stools, the black walls and blacker ceiling, were all its winking brightness shone upon." How conveniently symbolical this pile of rags and bones is. There is no such sign of poverty in the "poor but honest" home of the Toodles. Dickens could conceive of Edith selling herself for wealth. But could he face the possibility that prosperity might come from actual prostitution? Or, if that was rare in this period, at the very least, few prostitutes, still less their mothers, would have the symbolic requirements of novelists so much at heart as to put up with the inconvenience of piles of rags and bones on the floor.

v

In the last paragraphs we have considered what seem to me to be the book's main faults; but for his management of the sea symbol Dickens has generally had less than justice. Excessive attention has been focused on its most obtrusive appearance, at the time of Paul's death. Here Dickens failed, for a moment, to maintain the symbol's power and became sentimental. But only for a moment. There is nothing arbitrary about the genesis of the symbol. The sea is linked with a solid fact, the fact of commerce. London is a port; the interests of Dombey's firm range over the world; Walter Gay has to go to the West Indies; Captain Cuttle is an old seaman; Walter's uncle keeps a nautical shop; fashionable schools for young gentlemen are to be found, naturally enough, at Brighton which combines a faded air of royal occupation with a bracing climate—a combination irresistible in its appeal. All these are normal facts. And it is from these mundane realities, that Dickens, characteristically, built his symbolic arch. The first mention of the sea is brief but important:

> Thus, clinging fast to that slight spar within her arms, the mother drifted out upon the dark and unknown sea that rolls round all the world.

So Mrs. Dombey dies; she is known to the reader only by name, and she dies in the first chapter. Yet her death is the remote cause of much that follows. It is a death without characteristics; the death of every man. The connection between the sea and death soon becomes embedded in the mind of the child who was born when Mrs. Dombey died, and soon he begins to connect the sea with his own death.

Chapter 16, the death chapter, entitled " What the Waves were always Saying," is very difficult to criticise with balanced judgment. I suspect that some of those who are loudest in condemning it are angry with themselves for being moved by it. The river of time and the sea of eternity are, of course, time-honoured images, but they have a natural appropriateness which means that they can never be altogether exhausted. It is characteristic of Dickens to link this venerable symbolism with observation of detail, with the hypnotic effect of light dancing on the walls and ceilings of a sick-room.

As we have seen in an earlier chapter, it was virtually impossible for Dickens to describe the death of a child with full, unflinching seriousness; and Paul's last words, " The light about the head is shining on me as I go," can hardly be defended. This remark is an attempt to dispose of uncertainty about the nature of death and the hope of immortality by allowing Paul to give, while still living, a message from the other shore. It is, as it were, an attempt to turn him into Lazarus, without admitting that anything out of the ordinary has occurred. But the failure is momentary, and the grandeur of the whole design remains.

VI

To understand Dickens's middle and later works we need to remember always how he began—the gifted, irresponsible fantasist of *Pickwick Papers*, trusting to the inspiration of the moment, and finding his natural medium in the writing of monthly parts. But the euphoric magician had gifts of design and organisation which were at first entirely latent.

When he did make an attempt at a controlled masterpiece, he was obviously liable to over-compensate, and to allow parts of his plan to appear contrived. *Barnaby Rudge* and *Martin Chuzzlewit* reveal fragmentary signs of careful planning, but in *Dombey and Son*, for the first time, he followed an intelligible design throughout. The two leading ideas were pride, and the continuity of life. The first requires little comment; it reaches its climax when the apparently irresistible pride of Dombey meets the apparently immovable pride of Edith. Carker takes his place as the skilled manipulator of pride and Florence as the person who alone can cause the pride of each to melt. It is a sound, traditional scheme endowed with no exceptional psychological insight, but its interest lies in the transposition of an ancient feudal theme into a commercial society. The gloomy merchant's house in London beautifully represents the consequences of commercial pride, just as a decayed aristocratic mansion might represent the pride of a different era in the works of Scott.

But the balancing idea of the spontaneous continuity of life is more subtly treated, and in the end much more important. The key images of river, sea and railway all make a contribution. The idea is presented with a taut economy which is new to Dickens.

" On the brow of Dombey, Time and his brother Care had set some marks, as on a tree that was to come down in good time—remorseless twins they are for striding through their human forests, notching as they go—while the countenance of Son was crossed and recrossed with a thousand little creases, which the same deceitful Time would take delight in smoothing out and wearing away with the flat part of his scythe, as a preparation of the surface for his deeper operations."

But already in this first chapter we may wonder whether

the plan is not taking too obvious charge. It is true that Dombey would desperately desire a son, to continue the business and to maintain his sense of assimilation to an aristocracy committed to primogeniture. But would his dignity allow him to say to a hired woman, " Miss Florence was all very well, but this is another matter "? And we may have similar doubts when we find that the ship that takes Walter to the West Indies is called the *Son and Heir*, foreshadowing with irritating neatness, the story that follows, the loss of the ship, corresponding to the death of Paul, and Walter's destiny as Dombey's son-in-law and business heir. Melville or Hawthorne might carry this off, but such devices do not easily mingle with the more realistic tradition of English fiction.

But points like these only hint too obviously what the whole book conveys much more subtly, that as Miss Tox says at the time of Paul's death, " Dombey and Son was a daughter after all."

The Dombey doctrine, absurd when stated in cold blood, is yet the practical guide of millions of people. It is that one can and should dominate circumstances and mould destiny. Dombey presents this idea with a ponderous dignity, and his sister, Miss Chick, transposes it into a scatter-brained female form: commenting on Mrs. Dombey's death, she says, " I hope this heart-rending occurrence will be a warning to all of us, to accustom ourselves to rouse ourselves and to make efforts in time when they're required of us." And she urges Florence to conquer her father's deep-seated indifference with the simple formula: " Engage his attention, my dear." Florence knows better, she understands the weakness of the will to achieve its aims. Florence, with her endless waiting game, is essential to a book which shows destiny carelessly moulding those who try to mould destiny.

But perhaps it is in casual details that the author's sense

of inexorable continuity is best shown. Take, for instance, the sequel to Paul's death:

" There is not much business done. The clerks are indisposed to work; and they make assignations to eat chops in the afternoon, and go up the river. Perch the messenger stays long upon his errands; and finds himself in bars of public-houses, invited thither by friends, and holding forth on the uncertainty of human affairs. He goes home to Ball's Pond earlier in the evening than usual, and treats Mrs. Perch to a veal cutlet and Scotch ale." Then a day or two later, " There is sounder sleep and deeper rest in Mr. Dombey's house to-night, than there has been for many nights. The morning sun awakens the old household, settled down once more in their old ways. The rosy children opposite ran past with hoops. There is a splendid wedding in the church. The juggler's wife is active with the money-box in another quarter of the town. The mason sings and whistles as he chips P-A-U-L in the marble slab before him." Passages like this show Dickens triumphantly combining his innate sense of life's swarming vitality with his gradually acquired skill in design and the presentation of ideas, and so they represent a notable stage in his development.

Such passages ensure also that the symbolic treatment of continuity and change will not bear the taint of abstract schematic theorising. They provide an effective background of common life to the more intense emotions of Paul and Florence. Everywhere there is a contrast between the settled order of civilised life, and the unpredictable. Thus Paul's sea voices are contrasted with the clock in Blimber's academy, and Paul can tell the difference in the sound of the watches of the three doctors who visit him.

Clocks and watches, of course, represent the mysteries of life and death comfortably reduced to a human measure. But the waves and river are not just a symbol of the mysterious unpredictability of these things. They also, and even primarily, represent the inner voice which speaks to each man as he is dreaming alone. And no one knew better than Dickens that if this inner voice is sometimes pure and mysterious, it can also be self-deluding and materialistic. So Chapter 41, " New Voices on the Waves," is of cardinal importance, and shifts the balance of the whole book. For here Mrs. Skewton, like Paul, dies at Brighton within sight of the sea, but dies as she has lived, a materialist, rejecting any mystery in death, and bringing no hints of mystery to the survivors. The main problem raised by her death is appropriate to her materialism; it is the awkward social problem of how and where she is to be buried. By showing the negative side of the mystery in this way, Dickens strengthens our sense of its reality. In the same chapter, we hear what the waves say to Blimber and Feeder, the guardians of the "human clock" of classical instruction. " Doctor Blimber is heard to observe behind them as he comes out last, and shuts the door, ' Gentlemen, we will now resume our studies.' For that and little else is what the Doctor hears the sea say, or has heard it saying all his life." Mr. Feeder, his assistant, on the other hand, " plainly hears the waves informing him, as he loiters along, that Doctor Blimber will give up the business; and he feels a soft romantic pleasure in looking at the outside of the house, and thinking that the Doctor will first paint it, and put it into thorough repair." And to Mrs. Brown the sea brings merely a noise empty of significance. So the mystery of death, and of the continuity of life is linked with what each man in his heart considers most important, even if it is only Latin grammar, or the prospect of becoming a headmaster. Yet there remains something objective in the waves' message; and those who ignore it are impoverished or maimed. " So Edith's mother lies unmentioned of her dear friends, who are deaf to the waves that are hoarse with the repetition of their mystery, and blind to the dust that is piled upon the shore. . . ."

Here Dickens very amply repairs the partial failure in the death of Paul. In the railways he gave a fascinating and balanced study of continuity and change in social life. In the sea voices he produced a subtle and satisfying equivalent for the conflict and the mingling of subjective and objective in religious affairs.

8

David Copperfield

No book of Dickens is so difficult to assess fairly as *David Copperfield*. It was the author's own favourite; and, of course, it is very much closer to his own experience than any of his other works. This means that the impression of abounding life, in which the whole of Dickens's work is so rich, is particularly strong; but it also means that the subtle kinds of falsification, which beset him—sentimentality, cheap resentment, and unreal victories over half-imagined evils—all these and other faults are present in a virulent form. To strike a critical balance here is difficult: the book is certainly a readers' favourite, as well as the author's. It is vastly enjoyable both for the simple and the discriminating. Everybody can appreciate Mr. Micawber, but what can the critic say about him? All criticism naturally tends to concentrate on the topics about which the most interesting things can be said. No doubt these topics tend to coincide, in a rough and ready way, with the greatest literary achievements. But there are exceptions. To read of Mr. Micawber is, as Chesterton said, like receiving a blow in the face. It is a deeply-felt experience, but it is not susceptible of analytic description. It follows that any detailed critical discussion of *David Copperfield* will tend to be unbalanced because it is impossible to give appropriate space to Micawber.

It is certain that the book has been widely loved. I suspect also that, more than most of Dickens's works, it has been read with the same spirit that the author writ. A character like Micawber almost annihilates differences of intellect and education in the readers. And the whole easy, fond reminiscent tone, slightly tinged with self-mockery, and rather more strongly tinged with self-pity, is very attractive, at times, to everyone. *David Copperfield* answers a very common requirement with supreme—perhaps unequalled—appropriateness. It does so by means of two almost opposite qualities, by the incredible clearness of the nostalgic pictures it presents, and by its marked tendency to fantasy. That is, it continually evades the consequences of its own assumptions; it lacks the inner logic of Dickens's most distinguished works. The first point may be taken as obvious; to the second I return later.

II

When Dickens wrote *David Copperfield* he was in a sound position to take stock of the past and to face the bogies of his childhood and adolescence. His fame was established; the slight setback he had suffered at the time of *Martin Chuzzlewit* was forgotten. He was an institution; he was prosperous; and he had recently, in *Dombey and Son*, taken a big step on the path which was to make him a great artist as well. The extreme personal reticence and the touchiness of the past now seemed to him out of place. He was ready to tell his own story. Or was he?

Perhaps not altogether. It is obvious, of course, that the emotional identification of Dickens with David is very strong; and his readers were clearly encouraged to be aware of a close analogy between them. Trivial clues, like the use of his own initials in reverse, were interwoven into a more straightforward identification of careers. David, like Dickens, was a parliamentary reporter, who became a literary man. Dickens, like all great artists, had a way of fulfilling a number of disparate aims at once. And if he wanted to unburden himself of his secrets, and to present himself in a favourable light, he also knew very well that his devoted public were longing to know more about the personality and experience behind the mask of Boz; an autobiographical novel would increase his sales. But if Dickens had a strong urge to speak publicly of his life and hard times, he also had an urge to falsify them. He could never quite come to terms with his father's disgrace as a debtor, or his own "declassing" in the blacking factory. Hence his actual accounts of these things, and his fictional variations upon them in *David Copperfield* are alike characterised by an excessive emotional instability. He oscillated between indignation, self-pity, and reticence of the stiff-upper-lip English school. He was moved successively or even simultaneously by a desire to be admired for his extraordinary triumph over circumstances, a desire to be pitied as a childish outcast, and a desire to appear as a gentleman to whom education and literary culture came as a birthright. All these impulses were reflected in *David Copperfield*, and as they are incompatible, and also, as Dickens realised when he faced them squarely, not very dignified emotions, it is not surprising that at times a heavy sentimental smoke screen was needed. For a writer with these devious ends in view, or rather, not exactly in view, but half-concealed from himself, the advantages of the form of *David Copperfield* are obvious. He could speak in the first person, and enjoy all the pleasures of sentimental reminiscence. He could put in enough obvious clues to convince even his dullest readers that the book had a connection with his own life. He could give his hero a recent history corresponding to his own; he could repeat in *David Copperfield* the facts about himself that everybody knew, for instance, the fact that he had been a parliamentary reporter. He could thus without telling any untruth cause the public to assume that the earlier scenes also were drawn from his own experience. So indeed, at the emotional level, many of them were, but there were also a good many convenient alterations of fact, and some false trails.

The key question about *David Copperfield*—and there is no satisfactory answer to it—is " How far did he exorcise his early fantasies by examining them calmly from a mature point of view, and how far did he bolster up old fantasies and create new ones by adding new fuel to the fire of his self-pity? " So far as the book's deliberate plan goes, of course, great care is taken to present David's childish and adolescent naïvety from a distance, through mature adult eyes. Passages like this reveal such an intention clearly:

" I suppose history never lies, does it? " said Mr. Dick, with a gleam of hope.

" Oh, dear, no, sir! " I replied most decisively. I was ingenuous and young and I thought so.

But illusions like this are amiable failings and cost no effort to recall and admit. The criticism of David comes nearer to the author's personality when he is shown as a born actor, revelling in the tragic impression he is able to make on his schoolfellows at the time of his mother's death, or in his treatment as a budding young lawyer, of Barkis's will:

I felt myself quite a proctor when I read this document aloud with all possible ceremony, and set forth its provisions, any number of times to those whom they concerned. I began to think there was more in the Commons than I had supposed. I examined the will with the deepest attention, pronounced it perfectly formal in all respects, made a pencil mark or so in the margin, and thought it rather extraordinary that I knew so much.

The mockery which the mature David directs at his love for Dora is again something that need not have cost Dickens much. David's absurdity here is amiable, and, vastly exaggerated though it is, is derived from a very common experience to which it is no shame to confess. Even so, the self-mockery misfires a little. In the first place, he is a great deal more severe on the self-centred feminine immaturity of Dora than he is on his own failings. Dora's dreaminess reaches a point of real cruelty when she answers the penniless David's talk of a "crust well-earned" by stipulating that her dog must have his mutton chop every day punctually at twelve. David's forbearance in the face of this leaves us strongly biased in his favour, while the pseudo-literary romanticism of Miss Mills's journal (" Must not D.C. confide himself to the broad pinions of time? " etc.) makes David seem by far the most sensible of the three.

When David does smile at his own calf-love an uneasy facetious tone creeps in, and tends to inhibit any serious criticism: " Red Whisker pretended that he could make a salad (which I didn't believe), and obtruded himself on public notice. Some of the young ladies washed the lettuces for him, and sliced them under his directions. Dora was among these. I felt that fate had pitted me against this man, and one of us must fall." This sort of treatment might lead us to think that adolescent jealousy was part of an amusing game. David's faults can all be put down to a romantic immaturity. The self-criticism has no sting.

It is worth noticing that this superficial treatment of jealousy has its own nemesis. For when the real passion of jealousy appears it comes half-unnoticed by the author. It is dressed in the colours of righteous and altruistic feeling, and David's self-criticism is wholly absent. I mean, of course, the passages in which David contemplates a possible marriage between Agnes and Uriah Heep.

Uriah Heep is a puzzling and unsatisfactory character. There is a certain psychological insight in the original conception of him. He is a man deliberately trading on the moral confusions of others. Inability to distinguish between Christian humility and the social subservience of the lower orders was, we know, a common Victorian failing, and one which can be traced back to the origins of the serious English novel—to Richardson's *Pamela*. It is credible that a clever rogue starting with every social handicap as a charity boy should quickly detect this blind spot in the society around him, and trade on it. But his repellent physical nature is unfairly overstressed, and treated as if it were a moral failing. His damp, sweaty palm is not merely, like so many physical details in Dickens, exaggerated; it is presented as exactly what we should expect of such an ill-bred fellow. Physical repulsion, moral disapproval and class superiority are mingled, are boiled up together into a kind of broth where they become indistinguishable. And the indignation David feels about Uriah's wish to marry Agnes cannot possibly be put down to respect for her virtues. Uriah is called "a red-headed animal" so as to exploit the cheap horror of a possible sexual violation of the pure maiden. Here, in the midst of reading an important work of a very great novelist, we are astonished to find ourselves in the world of *Murder in the Red Barn*—but worse, because Dickens lacks the redeeming naïvety of such a work.

If the contempt for Uriah is partly a class-feeling, this leads us to consider the curiously ambiguous class position of David himself. His father is dead before he is born—a convenient arrangement in view of Dickens's feelings of shame about his own father; and it seems that everyone else in the book, during his adult years at least, is a little too conscious that he is a gentleman and confers honour by paying a visit. But this fault, if it is a fault, is largely neutralised by a powerful satirical comment on two variants of the gentlemanly code. It is an important moment in David's mental development when he warns Traddles not to lend anything to Micawber, and, when told that Traddles has nothing to lend, replies, " You've got a name, you know." This vision of Micawber, for the first time "in focus" is very effective. He is no longer a fantastic, lovable eccentric only—though he always remains that—he becomes a man who uses the gift of the gab to extract promises of money, and cheaply satisfies his gentlemanly honour by torrents of epistolary remorse.

The case of Steerforth is more complicated. Steerforth is really, it would seem, a thoroughly abandoned character from the first. He is already shown at his very worst while still at school in his treatment of Mr. Mell. His cruelty, then, combined with his insufferable upper-class vulgarity, make David's hero-worship seem much less touching than it is supposed to be. More important, it deprives the scene in which Steerforth begs David to think of him at his best, if circumstances should ever part them, of any background of momentous choice or moral struggle. Men of Steerforth's type would think little of the sin of seducing a fisherman's daughter. But despite this weakness, there is much psychological truth in parts of Steerforth's story. Chapter 22, in particular, in which Steerforth and David talk to Miss Mowcher, is a triumph. We see both David's naïve fascination at this extraordinary little woman, who knows all about the fashionable world, and Steerforth's lazy, morbid interest in her deformity. We see how her fashionable talk and the morbid interest she excites (and plays up to because her living depends on it) combine to make Steerforth less guarded than usual about shocking David's innocent susceptibilities. When Steerforth shows his contempt for the Peggottys and Ham and ordinary people generally, David performs a complicated, but perfectly credible mental juggling act, which allows him to pretend to himself that of course Steerforth does not mean all this, while he secretly enjoys the blasé, aristocratic flavour of his friend's worldliness. He is now on the way at last to realising how aimless and tedious is Steerforth's inner life, and is prepared for Miss Mowcher's explanations, which will show him how far removed from pity and respect is Steerforth's superficial kindness to her.

III

Everyone has noticed, I suppose, how close *David Copperfield* is to the traditional fairy story. Much of it is a day-dream, where pieces of gigantic good or evil fortune happen without cause or consequence, where each incident seems detached from every other. The Murdstones enter the scene like ogres; they fade away like a nightmare, and it is probable that no one ever acquired legal control of a child as quickly and easily as Betsy Trotwood did of David. Betsy Trotwood herself is perfectly in the tradition of the fairy godmother—omnipotent, wilful and kind. She has no human need to conform herself to reality. All her prejudices, some of which are cruel, are treated as admirable. Fairy godmothers have a right to them.

Peggotty's house belongs to fairytale and so does the account of Barkis going out with the tide. One has only to compare this last scene with the serious symbolic use of the sea in *Dombey and Son* to see the great difference. And,

moreover, *Dombey and Son* had already been written; the
Barkis episode is not the product of immaturity, but of a kind
of deliberate relapse to an earlier and less exacting method.
It is not just a study of local superstitions and of a child's
eager response to them. For the fact follows the superstition,
just as it does in fairy-tales. Throughout the book, there is
no real pressure of reality, no logic of cause and effect. We
are almost in Freud's territory of the omnipotence of
thought. David, employed in the wine firm, needs a kind
relative, money and education. He finds them. David
desires to marry Dora against her father's consent. He will
not relent, and Dora could never disobey him. So Dora's
father suddenly dies. Dora is the type of feather-brained
beauty who is only tolerable when she is very young, and
David needs to escape to the safe arms of his good angel,
Agnes. So Dora too dies, and, of course her beloved dog
drops dead at the same moment. Agnes's father must be
saved from the machinations of his partner, so Mr.
Micawber, of all people, must sedulously and snakily find
proof of all the partner's crimes. All the shrewd criticism
offered by the author of the Micawber routine of debt and
misery cannot hide the fact that the financial and professional
side of the novel is itself Micawberish. Something always
turns up at the last moment. And all the criticism of Dora's
feathery self-centredness cannot hide the fact that the book's
emotional life is largely Dora-ish. Difficulties and dangers
disappear like mist; and their main function seems to be
to give that quickened sense of joy and relief which follows
their miraculous removal.

These facts are clear; but it is not easy to assess them.
The design of the book seems to be, first to give a highly-
coloured vision of life through the innocent eye of childhood, and then to show the slow impact of reality and adult
standards on this vision. But the balance between the two

parts is never achieved. The mature David is at times hardly more than an overgrown childish David; and the author connives at his immaturity by giving so many of his dreams a solid substance afterwards. At first the fairytale atmosphere is appropriate, but the effect is bound to be spoilt when it creeps in unexpectedly in deliberately "mature" passages.

I suppose it is true to say that a fairy story should be either very naïve or very sophisticated. It should be either Mrs. Molesworth's *Cuckoo Clock* or Thomas Mann's *Holy Sinner*. Dickens, already in the process of developing into a great artist at this time, yet retained to the day of his death some extremely childish feelings and opinions. He was not the man to achieve either type of excellence. But one quality needed by the writer of fairy tales he did have in superabundant measure—the brooding imaginative force, which can endow material objects with demonic life. He could live among his own creations. This faculty, which no one, perhaps, has ever possessed in a higher degree than Dickens, makes the book impressive and memorable despite all its faults. Moreover, the occasional touches of true psychological insight (like the explanation why Micawber never borrowed money from David) stand out from the fairytale in splendid relief.

IV

The book's most unsatisfactory aspect is undoubtedly the fake autobiographical. It is difficult to criticise, because obviously any novelist has a perfect right to invent a fictional character partly like and partly unlike himself. But here we have something more than that. There are some incidents which make no sense at all in terms of the plot and of David's position in the world. But they become crystal clear as soon as they are seen as an attempt to exorcise or tame intractable and bitter memories. Take for instance, David's account of his fears when he was first taken to Dr. Strong's school in Canterbury. " But, troubled as I was, by my want of boyish skill, and of book-learning too, I was made infinitely more uncomfortable by the consideration that, in what I did know, I was much farther removed from my companions than in what I did not. My mind ran on what they would think, if they knew of my familiar acquaintance with the King's Bench Prison? Was there anything about me that would reveal my connection with the Micawber family—all those pawnings and sellings, and suppers—in spite of myself? "

Now David has no family connection with Micawber. He has merely paid to lodge in his house in a distant part of the country. He might expect, in the ordinary course of events, never to see Micawber again. And there is no disgrace attached to having had normal business transaction with a man who later becomes an insolvent debtor. Surely we are justified in saying that this incomprehensible fear only makes sense if it reflects the author's own feeling of disgrace about his father's sojourn in the debtors' prison.

After this we begin to notice other facts which point in the same direction—that the blacking factory is changed to the more gentlemanly counting-house in the wine trade. While David's father is conveniently dead the alien Miss Murdstone has to bear the weight of the childish resentment, which Dickens undoubtedly felt against his own mother, while David's mother is more sinned against than sinning.

Perhaps the most extraordinary example is the transformation of the sadistic schoolmaster Creakle of Salem House. " He had a delight in cutting at the boys, which was like the satisfaction of craving appetite." . . ." I am sure that when I

think of the fellow now, my blood rises against him with the
disinterested indignation I should feel if I could have known
all about him without ever having been in his power; but
it rises hotly because I know him to have been an incapable
brute, who had no more right to be possessed of the great
trust he held, than to be Lord High Admiral or Commander-
in-Chief—in either of which capacities it is probable that
he would have done infinitely less mischief." That is no
childish complaint; it is a balanced adult analysis. It is not
surprising that such a man should wish to be a magistrate
and to concern himself with the administration of prisons.
But we can only be astonished when we find that Creakle's
prison is a model one, and that David's bitter complaint
against it, strongly echoed by Dickens, is that it is too costly
and too comfortable. Creakle now admires and adores the
prisoners. That is odd enough; but it is odder still that
Creakle is not supposed essentially to have changed. There
is no conversion or repentance. His credulous and sub-
servient attitude to the prisoners is due to the same perverted
character he revealed long ago. Why? Of course because
Uriah Heep and Steerforth's servant Littimer are among the
prisoners. The urge to vengeance against them is very
strong. So the man who thwarts David's vengeful feelings by making his enemies so comfortable is treated as
cruel. This purely emotional link between the first and
second Creakle seems to be the only one. It would have
been easy to invent another character as governor of the
prison.

Now the type of self-pity shown in this strange illogical
identification is sinister. The natural and venial self-pity of
a man remembering boyhood sufferings is merging into the
self-pity of the adult denied his right to punish everybody
who has annoyed him. It is very close to violence and
tyranny. One recalls Auden's line in *Epitaph on a Tyrant*:

" When he cried, the little children died in the streets."
This prison scene is a very minor one; but it gives a very
important clue to what is wrong with the whole book.
David Copperfield goes bad at the point where retrospective
reverie merges into disingenuous self-justification, thirsting
for vengeance.

9

Bleak House

Bleak House begins, as everyone knows, in a fog. And probably most readers have felt that this was important. There is an obvious and explicit connection between this fog and the mental fog of the law courts. But there is also something more. The world of *Bleak House* is a world in which no problem is really faced, in which nothing is understood, in which the meaning of words has decayed. Hints of this come early: " Another ruined suitor, who periodically appears from Shropshire, and breaks out into efforts to address the Chancellor at the close of the day's business, and who can by no means be made to understand that the Chancellor is legally ignorant of his existence after making it desolate for a quarter of a century. . . ."

They are all in the same boat. Normal distinctions of judgment, intelligence, even of sanity, break down. The Lord Chancellor does not understand. Jo, the crossing sweeper, does not understand. The mad Miss Flite doesn't understand. Even the excellent Jarndyce completely mistakes the character of Harold Skimpole.

It is this universal threat of uncertainty, of course, that surrounds with an aura of horror the people who are generally agreed to be crazy. Miss Flite, with her " judgment on the Day of Judgment," Krook, with his insane parody of the

Lord Chancellor, are, in a sense, right. They estimate the probable working of the legal system more accurately than do the sensible men. Their madness can be seen as a window upon a strange world of sanity. Yet it is madness all the same. We are reminded of the mad characters in Jacobean plays. There is hardly a parallel in the Victorian period.

Yet all this was achieved without any sacrifice of that marvellous vividness in the presentation of physical objects and of peculiarities of behaviour, which Dickens had possessed from the first. The fog is at once the most actual and the most symbolical of all fogs.

By making some of the bitterest opponents of the legal system crazy, Dickens extended the range of his social criticism. He was very prone to fits of impotent irritation and superficial reforming zeal. Temperamentally, he may have been inclined to condemn all the abuses and anomalies of law in a lump as manifestly absurd. But in *Bleak House* he has passed beyond this point. In a world of such uncertainty even law courts may be suspected of having some positive value. However, this is revealed only gradually.

The point at which Dickens most obviously emerges from his habit of condemning authority and order without reservation is in the character of Skimpole. Skimpole is the answer to the question, which the younger Dickens would never have thought of asking: " What would Pickwick be like if he had no money? " Skimpole is portrayed with all the bitterness of personal disillusionment. Skimpole had, as it were, taken in Dickens himself, for he was peculiarly susceptible to the cant of a false generosity, as are most men, who, like him, are avaricious and ashamed of being avaricious. So Skimpole's talk has that peculiar note of being just too convincing to be true.

He had no objection to honey, he said, but he protested against the overweening assumptions of Bees. He didn't at all see why the busy Bee should be proposed as a model to him; he supposed that the Bee liked to make honey, or he wouldn't do it—nobody asked him. It was not necessary for the Bee to make such a merit of his tastes. If every confectioner went buzzing about the world, banging against everything that came in his way, egotistically calling upon everybody to take notice that he was going to his work and must not be interrupted, the world would be quite an insupportable place.

This passage comes in Chapter 8, which is called "Covering a Multitude of Sins." It is a packed and fascinating chapter, containing Mr. Jarndyce's attack on Wiglomeration and a study of the slow, self-righteous workings of official charity. The chapter achieves an extraordinary balance. It contains in miniature the forces which prevent the book as a whole from being just a cheap attack on the legal system. It is as if truth lay undetected in the midst of three kinds of error—official justice, official charity, and the bogus, informal good will of Skimpole, which can appear to the unwary eye so very like a viable alternative to the other horrors.

Skimpole's "good nature" is a kind of mirror-image of Jarndyce's. And it is significant that Jarndyce cannot see through him, while Esther easily does so. Skimpole stands as a monument to the hard-won fairness of mind of a man naturally prejudiced, the creation of a natural individualist unwillingly convinced of the need for routine, order and restraint. And this conviction came to its full development just when he was attacking the most absurd of all embodiments of these venerable ideas, the Court of Chancery. And on the opposite side, there is a moving, though much less noticeable monument to the same new feelings—the figure of Neckett, the bailiff, whom Skimpole named Coavins. Skimpole airily tells Jarndyce of his death: " Coavins has been arrested by the great bailiff. He will never do violence to the sunshine any more. Jarndyce goes to inquire about Neckett's orphaned children, and asks a local boy whether Neckett was industrious. " ' Was Neckett? ' says the boy. ' Yes, wery much so. He was never tired of watching. He'd set upon a post at a street corner, eight or ten hours at a stretch, if he undertook to do it.' " And Jarndyce comments, " He might have done worse, he might have undertaken to do it, and not done it."

Neckett represents routine, law and order in their basest, but still genuine form, just as the Jarndyce case itself shows them at their most pompous and absurd. And behind Neckett stands his family (" Three children. No mother. And that Coavinses' profession being unpopular. The rising Coavinses. Were at a considerable disadvantage."), and the unexpected forces of a more spontaneous life. It takes a big man to think of such things in the middle of an angry attack on legal forms. In view of all this even Mr. Kenge's fantastic justification of the Chancery system acquires a certain hollow dignity.

Neckett gives a hint of an important moment in Dickens's development. Even in *Oliver Twist* and in the early chapters of *David Copperfield* written not long before, evil had remained mainly an external threat. The lost solitary fugitive, hemmed in by dark powers, is (along with his fantastic humour) Dickens's main contribution to the mythology of literature. By this I mean the ideas which an author's name suggests to people who have hardly read him. But in *Bleak House* we get something new, only faintly fore-shadowed in a few scenes of *The Old Curiosity Shop* and *Barnaby Rudge*. The evil without does not only threaten and pursue; it now calls out to the evil within, and sometimes finds a ready answer. Consequently, a new value is seen to reside in the "undickensian" ideas of order, restraint, convention of which Neckett is the lowest and dullest, and therefore the most impressive representative. The correspondence of outer and inner evil appears first casually in tiny details:

" Although the morning was raw, and although the fog still seemed heavy—I say seemed, for the windows were so encrusted with dirt, that they would have made midsummer sunshine dim——" It occurs more strikingly in Chapter 14, where incurable delusion is placed squarely beside monstrous oppression. On one side are Miss Flite's birds, with their terrifying list of names, representing the practices and victims of Chancery—" Hope, Joy, Youth, Peace, Rest, Life, Dust, Ashes, Waste, Want, Ruin, Despair, Madness, Death, Cunning, Folly, Words, Wigs, Rags, Sheepskin, Plunder, Precedent, Jargon, Gammon and Spinach." (This has some claim to be called the best list in literature.) But in the same chapter and in the same house is Krook, the sham Chancellor, who won't allow himself to be taught to read, because someone might teach him wrong and " I'd rather trust my own self than another." Dickens had always been aware of obsessions, but usually in the past he had been concerned with their superficial humorous side. If we compare Mr. Dick's obsession with Krook's, the difference will be obvious. The satirical attack on the legal system is strengthened rather than weakened by this new balance, and new respect for order.

II

As we should expect, along with these new insights, a more complex vision of society was developing. Here *Bleak House* was not altogether a pioneer, for *Dombey and Son* had pointed the way. But the chief technical device by which this new vision is conveyed is strange. It is done by means of germs and infection. If Dickens succeeded, as I believe he did, in winning artistic power out of these intractable materials, it is surely a remarkable sign of greatness and originality.

It is obvious that the author intended to give symbolic force to the spontaneous combustion passage: " The Lord Chancellor of that Court, true to his title in his last act, has died the death of all Lord Chancellors in all Courts, and of all authorities in all places under all names soever, where false pretences are made, and where injustice is done. Call the death by any name Your Highness will, attribute it to whom you will, or say it might have been prevented how you will, it is the same death eternally—inborn, inbred, engendered in the corrupted humours of the vicious body itself— Spontaneous Combustion, and none other of all the deaths that can be died."

Powerful though this passage is in a way, I think we must agree that Dickens failed here. He achieved a more grotesque effect than he intended, and only made it worse by a pugnacious preface, which argued the precise medical accuracy of his symbolic structure. He was much more successful in a passage like this: " Then the active and intelligent . . . comes with his pauper company to Mr. Krook's, and bears off the body of our dear brother here departed, to a hemmed-in churchyard, pestiferous and obscene, whence malignant diseases are communicated to the

bodies of our dear brothers and sisters who have not departed;
... with every villainy of life in action close on death, and
every poisonous element of death in action close in life—
here, they lower our dear brother down a foot or two; here
sow him in corruption, to be raised in corruption: an
avenging ghost at many a sick bedside: a shameful testimony
to future ages how civilisation and barbarism walked this
boastful land together." Here he is using as a sign of moral
corruption a dim and dreary fact of the blue-books. He was
dealing with something very familiar in the every-day lives
of his readers, but something strikingly new as the material
of art. He was to develop this combination even more
memorably in *Our Mutual Friend*. He remains to this day
almost the only poet of industrial society.

III

Now we turn to a part of the novel which no one, I suppose,
regards as wholly satisfactory—the Dedlock story. Dickens
was trying here to incorporate a well-worn literary tradition
into a new type of art. The traditional melodramatic plot
with guilty secrets and long-lost heirs, like all popular and
traditional stories, embodies some deep human feelings—
notably a sense of the unexpectedness of life, and the
fortuitous character of advantages of wealth and education.
It is capable of reaching a high point of artistic development, as in *A Winter's Tale*. But for Dickens it had several
drawbacks. The tradition was nearing the end of its long
life when it came into his hands. A new version of it,
inaugurated, I suppose, by Balzac, and later developed in
America, was better fitted to the social background and to
the imaginative needs of the nineteenth century. I mean the
version where the fluctuations of wealth depend on business
hazards and the stock markets. So Dickens tried something

which is always very difficult—to give new life to a dying tradition. But some of his contemporaries, and indeed, juniors, George Eliot and Trollope, in particular, might have found it easier than he did, for they possessed a natural sympathy with the old world of rural privileges and obligations. Dickens had none; for him the squire was just a man who did no work. And so, though he presented Sir Leicester Dedlock as an honourable and high-spirited gentleman, and conveyed his opinions plausibly enough (civilisation tottering, etc.), he was unaware of any real influence for good or ill that such a man might have on his tenants and neighbours. It is characteristic of Dickens to tell us a great deal about Tulkinghorn, his man of business in London, and nothing about the way the estate was run.

But the fact remains that despite the unconvincing nature of Lady Dedlock's guilty secret, and her husband's comic opera obstinacy, something important was being attempted in the Dedlock story. It was a way of conveying something easy to state, and very difficult to grasp imaginatively, the corporate nature of society. The melodramatic plot is designed to reveal the interconnection between the wretches of Tom-all-alone's, and the ladies who furnish material for the fashionable intelligence. It is attempting in terms of plot and character to give what is conveyed by the key images of the spontaneous combustion of the body of the pseudo-Lord Chancellor, and the pollution of the atmosphere by the filthy dwellings of the poor. It is a strange experience to find these three things together—one a development of an antiquated theatrical tradition, one a naïve piece of Victorian pseudo-science, reminiscent of Zola's *Dr. Pascal*, and the third, air pollution, a grim fact which most novelists would have found utterly intractable for art. Taken together, they might be called a picture in miniature of the strangeness of Dickens's achievement.

IV

Dickens was wise to choose simultaneously a number of different ways of presenting his view of corporate society, so difficult as it is to apprehend imaginatively. It is an idea we need to be shown, not told. Of course, beyond the three methods of presentation just mentioned, there were others, more obvious. Take, for instance, the case of Krook, the imitation Lord Chancellor. Without the support offered by the Dedlock story and the germ-dirt image, Krook might be taken as a fantasy, merely ornamental. But once the idea is established that society is a seamless fabric, Krook can take his full part as a grotesque illustration of a sober truth. Dickens was very cunning here. For he divested himself of responsibility for the fantasy. Krook in his madness is deliberately aping the real Lord Chancellor; so that the obvious absurdity of the comparison between them appears as a strange foible of human nature, objectively reported. " I go to see my noble and learned brother pretty well every day. He don't notice me, but I notice him." Once this element of deliberate burlesque by Krook is established, we are free to notice something else—Krook's profound inner conformity, deeper than anything he is aware of, to the spirit of the constitution. " Read," says Tony to Mr. Guppy. "He'll never read. He can make all the letters separately, and he knows most of them separately when he sees them; he has got on that much under me; but he can't put them together," and, " But his whole stock from beginning to end, may easily be the waste paper he bought it as, for anything I can say. It's a monomania with him, to think he is possessed of documents." Here Krook is unconscious of the part he is playing, that of the legal system, burdened with precedents, unable to see life for disjointed facts. The combination of deliberate parody and this pervasive unguessed likeness is impressive. And if the incident of the spontaneous combustion is, on the whole, a failure, it is largely redeemed by what immediately follows, the inquest. Never has the power of law to discover facts and miss realities been better conveyed. Yet even here balance is maintained. If Skimpole prevents us sneering too easily at respectable routine, Chadband is there to give us pause when we laugh at legal verbiage. Chadband, like Skimpole, is not an attack on the vices of other people, but on a corrupt form of one of the author's own qualities. Chadband shows us what happens when sentimental goodwill congeals into an icy rigidity. And this leads to my last and most important point. In *Bleak House*, while retaining to the full his wonderful and violent energy, and swarming invention, he came near to that great and perhaps unattainable target of being fair. No one, reading *Nicholas Nickleby* would have believed it possible.

Hard Times—
Dickens's Masterpiece?

Dr. Leavis has performed a valuable service by focusing attention on *Hard Times*, an important and neglected work. Those of us who do not quite agree with him about its quality are nevertheless grateful.

The leading idea of the book is proclaimed in the contrast between its subject, industrial society, and the titles of its three sections—Sowing, Reaping and Garnering. The intention, carried out at times with great subtlety and at times with a rather weary obviousness, was to show inherent life and growth conquering theory and calculation. This approach tends to break down the stock distinctions between town and country, between industry and agriculture, between science and intuition. From the first brilliant description of the factory world, where the elephants' heads represent the movements of machinery, the factory is treated as a living thing. Thus industrial smoke is linked with the horrors of hypocrisy and deception. " A blur of soot and smoke, now confusedly tending this way, now that way, now aspiring to the vault of Heaven, now murkily creeping along the earth, as the wind rose and fell, or changed its quarter: a dense formless jumble, with sheets of cross light in it, that showed nothing but masses of darkness: Coketown in the distance was suggestive of itself, though not a brick of it could be seen." And in a notable passage the fire of the furnaces is compared to the fire of human passions. When she is considering Bounderby's proposal, Louisa is asked by her father, " Are you consulting the chimneys of the Coketown works? " and she replies, " There seems to be nothing there but languid and monotonous smoke. Yet when the night comes, Fire bursts out."

Coketown and its people are living mysteries, not facts. The process of inner growth is never absent from the author's mind. It dominates even casual phrases: " to pretend . . . that they went astray wholly without cause, and of their own irrational wills, was to pretend that there could be smoke without fire, death without birth, harvest without seed." This, in part, is the meaning of Stephen Blackpool's fall into the disused mine, which causes his death. The creature of industrial society, the mine, does not cease to influence events when it is uncontrolled and forgotten—a point which Stephen's own words underline: " When it were in work, it killed wi'out need; when 'tis alone, it kills wi'out need."

Now it seems that two of the three main targets at which Dickens directed his criticism, were well chosen. Bounderby and Harthouse, each in his odd, inverted way, illustrate the principle of inner life and growth. Bounderby's story of character and industry triumphant is a sham; and his mock humility about being brought up in the gutter is a form of snobbery and pride. His relations with Mrs. Sparsit perfectly illustrate the real source of his feelings and his lies. The important point is that the low "down-to-earth" materialistic attitude takes its origin in an idealistic illusion. Harthouse, on the other hand, has adopted the dogmas of political economy out of boredom, out of that weary assumption of originality, which is always a mark of dullness of mind. (How well Dickens understood this *avant-garde* type. Gowan in *Little Dorrit* is a different and equally interesting version of it.) Also Harthouse knows in advance that the devotees of political economy will be secretly impressed with his upper-class connections. Therefore he will carry more weight in their councils than he would in circles more accustomed to enjoying aristocratic support. His pose is one of cynicism. " The only difference between us and the professors of virtue or benevolence, or philanthropy—never mind the name—is, that we know it is all meaningless, and say so; while they know it equally and will never say so." But this sincere-insincerity is itself insincere. He has no real interest in the cynical principles of the political economists; his cynicism is only an attractive line. He is the ancestor of a long line of "brutally frank and courageously outspoken" publicists of the twentieth century; and it can be fairly claimed that Dickens may well have been the first person to understand and analyse the type.

Altogether it is a beautifully-planned contrast between Bounderby and Harthouse. But the third term is surely weaker than Dr. Leavis allows. Gradgrind seems to belong to the world of pure moral fable—which in its main outlines *Hard Times* most certainly is not. So we are uneasy whenever Gradgrind has dealings with Bounderby and Harthouse. They are not the same kind of creature at all, and so can only communicate, as it were, through the author's mind. And so there is no reserve of dramatic force to play with at the time of Gradgrind's conversion; the conversion itself, accordingly, is almost trivial.

Of course, the atmosphere of the moral fable, or even of the fairytale is introduced deliberately at times. We cannot doubt that when we read a sentence like this: " Stephen, whose way had been in a contrary direction, turned about, and betook himself as in duty bound to the red brick castle of the giant Bounderby." It is deliberate, but is it always judiciously used? Neither Bounderby nor Blackpool really deserves this aura of fairytale. Each has his own psychological truth; and each has characteristics which could not occur in any pre-industrial society.

There is a similar difficulty about the circus. Dr. Leavis says, most aptly, of the scene where Sleary finally points the book's moral: " Reading it there we have to stand off and reflect at a distance to recognise potentialities that might have been realised elsewhere as Dickensian sentimentality. There is nothing sentimental in the actual fact." The crucial importance of Mr. Sleary and the circus is obvious. The circus is at the beginning and the end. From it comes Sissy Jupe to save the Gradgrind family; and Tom, the disgraced product of a politico-economical education returns to it to make his escape.

But here again we meet the difficulty, are we reading a fable or a novel? In a semi-realistic work of this sort we can hardly be satisfied with the circus as a simple undifferentiated alpha and omega, like Kafka's castle or the lake from which Arthur's sword appeared and to which it returned. We are bound to look for some positive wisdom in Mr. Sleary and I cannot help feeling that Dr. Leavis is too enthusiastic when he speaks of "the solemn moral of the whole fable, put with the rightness of genius in Mr. Sleary's asthmatic mouth." Sleary belongs, of course, to a long tradition of the wise or holy fool. To speak of genius here is surely to place Sleary among the finest representatives of this tradition, to put him in the company of the Fool in *Lear* and Dostoevsky's Myshkin. He will scarcely stand the comparison; and the passage Dr. Leavis quotes will hardly support his claim:

" Thquire, you don't need to be told that dogth ith wonderful animalth."

" Their instinct," said Mr. Gradgrind, "is surprising."

" Whatever you call it—and I'm bletht if I know what to call it"—said Sleary, "it ith athtonithing. The way in which a dog'll find you—the dithtanthe he'll come."

" His scent," said Mr. Gradgrind, " being so fine."

" I'm bletht if I know what to call it," repeated Sleary, shaking his head, " but I have had a dogth find me, Thquire. . . ."

It is generally acknowledged by Dr. Leavis and others that the Trade Union scenes are not satisfactory; though Dickens achieved one stroke of prophetic insight, when, in Bounderby's interview with Blackpool, he showed the sub-conscious sympathy between owners and Trade Unions linked against individualistic workers.

The parallel between Bounderby's and Blackpool's matrimonial troubles is unconvincing; and one feels that probability, psychology and everything else had been sacrificed to symmetry. The last chapter summarises in a few hundred words events which might fill a whole novel. Here Dickens's sense of the superiority of life to fact, which is the guiding star of the novel, up to this point, seems ironically to have deserted him. Gradgrind could almost have written the chapter himself.

There are then, it seems to me, sound reasons against considering *Hard Times* a masterpiece. But it remains a work of great distinction, which performed for the first time the very important imaginative task of integrating the factory world into the world of nature and of humanity. And I end with a quotation designed to show this process at work. It is like a new pastoral tradition miraculously beginning, in which the Industrial Revolution can really share: " They walked on across the fields and down the shady lanes, some-times getting over a fragment of a fence so rotten that it dropped at a touch of the foot, sometimes passing near a wreck of bricks and beams overgrown with grass, marking the site of deserted works. They followed paths and tracks, however slight. Mounds where the grass was rank and high, and where brambles, dockweed, and such like vegetation, were confusedly heaped together, they always avoided; for dismal.stories were told in that country of the old pits hidden beneath such indications."

I I

Little Dorrit

" The world has narrowed to these dimensions, Arthur."—
Mrs. Clennam.

We have already seen how the idea of prison dominates
Little Dorrit, and how prison becomes an image of society
as a whole; and we have noted that the image became more
powerful and more general because the book's chief prison,
the Marshalsea, no longer existed. The fact is important,
because it removes the book at once from the ranks of
reformist propaganda. It is no use calling for the abolition
of the debtors' prison; it has already gone, and, in Dickens's
view, the condition of the country, which that prison
epitomised, remains much the same.

So, instead of speaking again of the prison, I wish to
concentrate attention here on the various means of escape,
mental and physical, which the story offers, and to show
how all, or almost all, prove to be illusory. The two most
obvious ways of escape are through money and travel, the
natural opposites, so to speak, of confinement in prison for
debt. But Dorrit's new life of wealth leaves him very little
changed. In his prosperity he is gentlemanly in a haughty
sort of way, but so he was as Father of the Marshalsea. He
is still quick to seize on imaginary affront, still restlessly

jealous of his dignity, still ashamed of his daughter's more mundane activities. His final relapse in his last illness to the actual phrases proper to the Father of the Marshalsea only signalises a fact always implicit. The case of Merdle and wealth is even more obvious. His money gives him no grasp of affairs, no real power. He is a tool of interests that he does not understand. He is hustled into a social position that he cannot enjoy. He is a terrifying figure, *because he is not a villain*. He is at the apex of the financial structure, and yet seems to have no free will. In this he is an extreme case only of the condition of all the characters, a condition which is responsible for its profound (as opposed to superficial, " London-grimy") gloom. The abounding energy of the early Dickens characters, their multiple freedom of choice, aptly illustrated by Pickwick, free as air, travelling where he liked, or by Nicholas Nickleby, triumphant by his virtue and energy over enormous obstacles—all this is now buried. Travel has become a dreary purposeless compulsion, as in the claustrophobic scene in the inn on the St. Bernard Pass at the beginning of Part II. Clennam is an aimless wanderer through the streets of London on Sundays. Half the time he is going nowhere, moving like a clockwork toy. But Clennam and Little Dorrit herself do act a little, do show signs of the freedom of the will. Merdle is the central representative of the general powerlessness. Round him are grouped a curious collection of unnamed professional men, with trade titles like bar and bishop. Their anonymity is significant.

When we look back upon the swarming life of Dickens's early works, and even of *Bleak House*, only three or four years before *Little Dorrit*, we might be tempted, quite erroneously, to diagnose boredom or failing invention. But these new characters are anonymous because they are all flies on the chariot-wheels of destiny, crying out, " What a dust do I make." At this point we can gain assistance from *Dickens at Work* in which Professor Butt and Mrs. Tillotson have analysed the genesis of the book as revealed in the author's notebooks. He had in mind originally the title *Nobody's Fault*, a phrase which still occurs here and there in the finished work. The idea contained in the phrase is still dominating. The sufferings of Bleeding Heart Yard are unknown to the Circumlocution Office. The terrible, destructive blamelessness of Government is beautifully symbolised when an innocent and helpless foreigner is run down by the Government mail coach.

Dickens had always been fond of mystery, concealment and coincidence, but here we have, perhaps for the first time, something different, a general mystery, a sense of a mass of unknowable people and facts surrounding the soluble mysteries of the plot. " The long dusty roads and the interminable plains were in repose—and so deep a hush was on the sea, that it scarcely whispered of the time when it shall give up its dead." In the centre of a group of nameless people, distinguished only by their professional titles, and in the centre of a far larger mass of miserable city dwellers whose lurking presence is finely suggested (particularly in Chapter 14) stands Merdle. He has a name, but hardly a recognisable face, and he is gloomier and more terrible than the others because he alone realises the insignificance of his great position and the irrelevance of the adulation he receives. While they chatter on, he marches on to financial collapse and moral despair. It is said that Merdle was drawn from a famous swindler, and Dickens himself gave a hint to this effect in his introduction, but Merdle is much nearer to being a helpless victim. It is a very neat touch that the richest man in England has to borrow the knife with which he kills himself—a perfect indication of spiritual bankruptcy.

It is tempting, of course, to moralise upon all this, to

suggest that this new and exaggerated distrust of the power of the human will was the nemesis awaiting the exaggerated optimism, the cheerful determination to put the world to rights in five minutes, which is to be found in *Pickwick Papers.* But while we are actually reading *Little Dorrit,* such considerations hardly arise. We are carried along by the tremendous artistic power with which Dickens presents his myth of human weakness.

II

The myth is fortified by a series of ingenious parallels between the microcosm of the Marshalsea and the world outside. Thus the ineffectiveness of Merdle's millions is paralleled by the touching incident of the turnkey, trying to make his will.

> " Stop a bit," said the turnkey. " Supposing she was tender-hearted, and they came over her. Where's your law for tying it up then? "
>
> The deepest character whom the turnkey sounded, was unable to produce his law for tying such a knot as that. So, the turnkey thought about it all his life, and died intestate after all.

The ethos of the Barnacle clan, who rule the Circumlocution Office, and almost rule the country, is reflected by the words of Mrs. Chivery, the wife of the Marshalsea's lock-keeper, "a prudent woman, she had desired her husband to take notice that their John's prospects of the lock would certainly be strengthened by an alliance with Miss Dorrit, who had herself a kind of claim upon the College. . . ."

And the Chiverys' attitude to the exalted position of the Dorrits in prison life is similar to Meagles's reverence for the splendid but useless Barnacles. Dorrit and the Barnacles share the enjoyment of an engrained reverence, so traditional that no one troubles to ask about its cause. Dorrit's marvellous system of combining begging with patronising arrogance, is akin to the Barnacles' depredations of public funds for the benefit of their needy relatives.

In treating the whole difficult subject of class and social distinctions, Dickens had become both more gentle and more pessimistic than his earlier self, and than the majority of other novelists. Consider, for instance, the following speech of Mr. Meagles:

" A Barnacle is he? *We* know something of that family, eh, Dan? By George, they are at the top of the tree, though! Let me see. What relation will this young fellow be to Lord Decimus now? His Lordship married in seventeen ninety-seven, Lady Jemima Bilberry, who was the second daughter by the third marriage—no! There I am wrong! That was Lady Seraphina—Lady Jemima was the first daughter by the second marriage of the fifteenth Earl of Stiltstalking with the Honourable Clementina Toozellem. Very well. Now this young fellow's father married a Stiltstalking. . . ."
In some ways this is a very ordinary passage, and we do not have to go very far, even now, to hear the like of it. But there is a concealed sting in its ordinariness. For Meagles is an unusually kind and friendly person, who is mainly ruled by common sense. The youthful Dickens would have given such a speech to some ridiculous parasite of an incredible aristocrat like Lord Frederick Verisopht. An aberration of the few is transformed into an infection which spares no one. Then in the words " We know something of that family," Meagles is appealing to the experience shared by his friend Doyce and himself, who have been perpetually thwarted by these same Barnacles in their public capacity. But he switches without a pause to an awed social respect for the family whose incompetence he knows so well. His generous but

commonplace mind is incapable of permitting any inter-
action between social adulation and professional contempt,
and Dickens suggests that, so long as Meagles remains
typical the inefficiency of Government remains inevitable.

Of the Barnacles themselves and the Circumlocution
Office it is difficult to give a balanced account. And they are
so obviously, and yet so brilliantly funny, that argument and
discussion about them might seem to be beside the point.
But there is a good deal of serious social criticism contained
in those hilarious pages. Here, for instance, is a valid point
about the relation between the elected government and the
permanent Civil Service. " Every new premier and every
new government, coming in because they had upheld a
certain thing as necessary to be done, were no sooner come
in than they applied their utmost faculties to discover how
not to do it." And here is a serious criticism of the technique
of the parliamentary answer which need not be satisfactory
because no one really knows what the facts are: " Then
would he come down to that house with a slap upon the table,
and meet the honourable gentleman foot to foot. Then
would he be there to tell that honourable gentleman, that,
the Circumlocution Office was not only blameless in this
matter, but was commendable in this matter, was extollable
to the skies in this matter. Then would he be there to tell
that honourable gentleman, that, although the Circumlocution Office was invariably right and wholly right, it was
never so right as in this matter. . . ." But these are fairly
simple points, and there is a more delicate observation of
English manners, in the curious blend of formality and
informality, of traditional flummery, everyday common-
sense, and the "old-boy net," in the behaviour of the young
Barnacle whom Clennam meets in the office. He first
insists on the need for an appointment, and makes all sorts
of difficulties about the technique of getting a form to apply

for a form to be granted an appointment, but at the same time he talks in that colloquial, friendly style which England expects of her great men. " You really are going it at a great pace, you know," he says, and " Upon my soul, you mustn't come here saying you want to know, you know." But he weakly and kindly concludes by sending Clennam to see his father at his own house where any normal conscientious civil servant might expect to be free of public business. There is a subtle flavour of easy, friendly cynicism in all this talk of forms of procedure. The Barnacles are not narrow officials bound by rules. Family and education are the real basis of their careless power. They use books of rules as mere gestures which can be forgotten later. And all this, of course, makes it more difficult to attack them. A reasoned attack on the rules will invariably be met by the answer that the rules are not really observed, just as to this day the suggestion that it is unfitting for the Prime Minister to appoint Anglican bishops is always met with two unanswerable arguments, first that the Prime Minister does not really appoint them at all, and second that you get better bishops by his appointment than in any other way.

And so the Barnacles are not unfeeling bureaucrats; they are lazy, humane, selfish, privileged people, sheltering behind a weak barricade of minutes and forms. Incompetence, irritation, even kindness (as when the young Barnacle visits Clennam in prison) are continually breaking through. Dickens was doing something important here, he was showing how all this lovable absurdity, which he loved too perhaps, could have consequences that were harsh and irrevocable.

The function of the Circumlocution Office in the book's plan was to present an official version of the recurring idea of "no escape." Everyone is beating their hands against the walls of a prison. The office is one wall, and it is a wall made of feather beds, endlessly yielding but impossible to change. It is Kafka's "they" in familiar English dress—an unequalled achievement. But George Orwell has drawn attention to another aspect of the matter in which Dickens does not show up well. Orwell seems to me to overstress Dickens's ignorance of work. Clennam and Doyce are not unconvincing portraits of business men who understand work. But Orwell was surely right in saying that Dickens's criticism was entirely negative. He wrote as an artist, as a spectator, never as a citizen. He simply refused to recognise that government was necessary, and that no one has ever devised a way of excluding tedious routines from the business of government. As an artist and an entertainer he was above all these things. The startling, yet inescapable conclusion is that in this he was very like his own Henry Gowan. He is making fun of everything because he has contracted out of the normal routines of life.

Of course, the likeness is fortuitous and partial, and in no way affects the satirical justice of the portrait of Gowan himself. Gowan's story illustrates the danger of confusing honesty with cynicism, and truthfulness with malice. His modesty is a form of pride, for it is always saying, " If I, in my fortunate position, am not satisfied, while you, of course, envy me, how huge must my real desires and merits be." Civilisation and urbanity here come to mean only being insulated against the primary feelings. The case of Gowan shows with an insight that the early Dickens could not have attained that this pseudo-detachment is a subtle kind of worldliness, and that in a world of "no escape," escapism was no escape at all.

In the stifling atmosphere of "no escape" people are of course strongly impelled to patronise each other, and to try and compensate for ever being superior to circumstances by being obviously superior to human beings. There are many kinds of patronage, the Barnacle kind depends on an agreed social status, and a bogus English mystique of government —not a set of rules which an outsider might learn, but an inherited knowing of the ropes. There is the patronage, too, of Mrs. General, the governess-companion to the Dorrits in their later affluence. She compensates for her lonely, subordinate position by etiquette and correctness, which she confuses with class superiority. The Dickens of whom it had so often been said that he could not draw a gentleman, had by now developed a fine ear for class differences; he knew very well the distinction between the faded snobbish genteelism of Mrs. General and the real voice of the English upper classes, slangy and superficially friendly—" You really are going it at a great pace, you know." Mrs. General's character, social position and obsessive fears are all very neatly summed up in the scene where she refuses to discuss with Mr. Dorrit the amount of her remuneration. She even refuses to admit that she has been paid for her services, but is careful, in the course of the same conversation to secure a rise of thirty-three per cent.

But of course the subtlest version of patronage is to be found in Mr. Dorrit himself. To get the full flavour of its luxuriant development, it is necessary to go back to the description of his first appearance in prison in Chapter 6. He was then an amiable and helpless middle-aged gentleman, "well-looking though in an effeminate style; with a mild voice, curling hair and irresolute hands—rings upon the fingers in those days—which nervously wandered to his trembling lip a hundred times, in the first half-hour of his acquaintance with the jail." He addresses the turnkey humbly, and the turnkey thinks of him as a child. Such is his original nature, and if he had had a competent financial adviser, he could have remained mild and submissive. But the disgrace of the prison leads to a drastic over-compensation. He controls his gentlemanly distaste for accepting gifts of money by weaving a fantasy of his power and influence as the Father of the Marshalsea; and even comes to imagine that the money he receives is no more than a partial repayment for the favours he has conferred on others. The symbolic exorcisation of his disgrace is solemnly performed upon the head of Nandy. " Mr. Dorrit was in the habit of receiving this old man, as if the old man held of him in vassalage under some feudal tenure. He made little treats and teas for him, as if he came in with his homage from some outlying district where the tenantry were in a primitive state. . . . When he mentioned him, he spoke of him casually as an old pensioner. He had a wonderful satisfaction in seeing him and in commenting on his decayed condition after he was gone. It appeared to him amazing that he could hold up his head at all, poor creature. " In the Workhouse, sir, the Union; no privacy, no visitors, no station, no respect, no speciality. Most deplorable! "

It is typical of Dorrit that he should only reveal his long-standing knowledge that his daughter has to work for her living and his, when the news of his new wealth and freedom arrives, and he is in no need, for the moment, of sacrifices to his pride. Though, in his new position of splendour Mr. Dorrit remains touchy on the subject of class, we may suppose that he is cured of this deadly desire to compensate by patronising. But by a brilliant touch, patronage is transposed into another key, when he becomes alarmed about his health.

" Your uncle wanders very much, Amy." . . . " He is less —ha—coherent and his conversation is more—hum—broken, than I have—ha, hum—ever known. Has he had any illness since I have been gone? "

" No, Father."

" You—ha—see a great change in him, Amy? "

" I had not observed it, dear."

" Greatly broken," said Mr. Dorrit. " Greatly broken.
My poor, affectionate failing Frederick! Ha. Even taking
into account what he was before, he is—hum—sadly
broken! "

Any weakness in himself by now causes him to seek out
or invent a worse weakness of the same kind in others.
Nandy protected him from his dread of poverty and debt,
Frederick protects him from his fears about his own health
and approaching death. And this is more than a personal
idiosyncrasy. His daughter Fanny avenges herself much
more violently on the Sparkler and Merdle families for her
own social disgrace of the prison years. There is another, yet
more perverse operation of the same principle in the story
of Miss Wade and Tattycoram. When the world is a prison
the prisoners are liable to hit out at random.

In the plethora of roads marked " No thoroughfare," the
religious solution is not seriously considered. Such religion
as there is in the book is a kind of parody, and is powerfully
associated with the dominant claustrophobic atmosphere.
Mrs. Clennam sits for ever in her unchanging room, bitterly
reading her bible; and the English Sunday, so vividly
evoked in Chapter 3, is like a series of blank walls closing in.

It is true that Dickens occasionally pauses in his con-
demnations of Mrs. Clennam's type of religion in order to
disclaim any intention of attacking religion itself. But these
interludes find no echo in the action of the novel. They
remain *obiter dicta*, easily forgotten; and the reader is left
with the impression that while religion may be all right in
theory, it is generally evil in its practical working. The
gospel overtones, so prominent, for instance, in *Oliver Twist*
and *Great Expectations* are absent. Little Dorrit herself is

much nearer to some Pelagian or Rousseauist conception of natural virtue than to sanctity.

It would seem that for Dickens feelings were much stronger than beliefs. There seems to be no evidence of fundamental changes in his beliefs at any time in his life. He held to a loose, philanthropic, mildly anti-clerical Anglicanism, with more or less concealed Unitarian tendencies. But it would seem that he regarded religion as separate from the normal process of life—a kind of reserve area of feeling, a repository of pure and noble sentiments and of kindly moral impulses. So, if he was depressed or worried, or if his imagination was darkened, as in writing *Little Dorrit*, he tended to assume, probably without any conscious calculation, that religious thoughts were not appropriate to the situation. The " De Profundis " was notably lacking from his religion. Hence, no doubt, in part, the failure of some of his death scenes, which he felt it a duty to make pious, and was therefore impelled to make too nice. So it is that here and in *Our Mutual Friend*, two of his finest and gloomiest books, the religion, which he sincerely held, was the great absentee.

III

So far we have said nothing of the road of escape from the book's many prisons which was generally for Dickens the most important of all, the road through the solidarity of family life. Now it is true that even in his early and more cheerful books, family life often proves unsatisfactory; stock comic ideas of the henpecked husband are prominent, and, as we have seen, the family as a group predominates over the basic marital or parental affection. But in *Little Dorrit* family affections are subject to a more disquieting and more radical distortion than ever before.

The dominating impression is one of emotional impotence. The characters are haunted either by an inability to feel, or by an inability to express or act upon their feelings. Clennam, with his lonely depressed wanderings, his failure to compete with the hard and specious Gowan, his incomprehension of Little Dorrit's feeling for him, or indeed of his own for her—Clennam sets the tone for all the others. But the strangest and most significant effect derives from the confusion over Little Dorrit's age. When her life is first described in detail, we are told that she is twenty-two. But she looks like a child, her smallness is continually insisted upon, and in some ways she thinks and feels as a child.

The innocent child was always a stock Dickensian device for setting off the cruelty of the adult world. But Little Nell and Oliver Twist really are children. Reflecting on Little Dorrit's history, one would suppose that her life of early hardship and responsibility, the need to take the place of a dead mother, and the childish incompetence of her father would hasten the attainment of an adult outlook. But, however improbable it may be, the ambiguity about her age is extraordinarily appropriate to the book's pattern. It means that Clennam's feelings about her will be ambiguous and frustrated, that the damp, uncertain, depressing prison atmosphere will extend even to love between the sexes. It is true that Clennam does finally marry her, but it is a wedding at the prison gates, and it takes place under the cloud of imprisonment for debt.

Clennam's imprisonment is a most interesting improbability. It does not merely illustrate the imposing respectability of the Merdle façade, for Clennam, experienced, cautious and pessimistic would be one of the last people to be deceived. There is no doubt that Marshalsea has a half-concealed attractiveness for him, shown more openly for a moment when he says: " I would rather be taken to the

Marshalsea than any other prison." This attraction is partly due to the Marshalsea's long association in his mind with Little Dorrit, partly to a proud refusal to beg for favours. In any case, it gives Little Dorrit the opportunity to end as she began by ministering to the prisoners of the Marshalsea; and the shock of experiencing real imprisonment for the first time, helps Clennam to escape at last from uncertainty about his confused and ambiguous feelings. But there is no happy ending. An atmosphere of failure and frustration still lingers about this marriage at the prison gates. For Clennam has only come to appreciate his feelings for Little Dorrit when he has been disgraced and at last needs her practical help. This is presented as an irredeemable moral failure, for he should have given her his love when he was strong and she was weak. So it is that Little Dorrit's ambiguous age and Clennam's nervous distrust of his own emotions contribute to an ending thoroughly in keeping with the book's portentous, careworn movement.

There is nothing here to relieve the dominant impression of twisted and wasted emotions. Even the familiar Dickensian "character," that bulked so large in the early books, has here taken the sinister (though still very amusing) form of Mr. F.'s aunt. There is the curious story of Tattycoram and Miss Wade, which seems to combine a suppressed homosexual element with a study of the resentment that can be caused by kindness. There is the unexpectedly irrevocable separation of the spoilt Pet from her parents. There is Flora Finching, a walking satire on nostalgia and tender memories. There is a powerful sense of the pains of solitude. Above all, there is the deadly habituation of the Dorrit family to the kindness and endless patience of Amy or Little Dorrit. " She is a very good girl, Amy," says Mr. Dorrit. " She does her duty." And he dies, knowing no better.

Yet, in the end it would be wrong to suggest that *Little*

Dorrit was a work of unrelieved gloom. Artistic achievement wrought out of misery and boredom is extraordinarily rare and difficult. Tragedy and disaster are, by comparison, tractable materials. There are numerous pitfalls, and two, in particular, have claimed many literary victims, cynicism and the decline of righteous indignation into ill-tempered and egoistic petulance. In view of this, we shall be driven to agree, I think, that the gentleness of Little Dorrit is an artistic necessity, even though there may be a sentimental streak in the treatment of her ambiguous age and the sexual-cum-fatherly feelings of Clennam about her. And she and Clennam, in their common gentleness, are not altogether alone in a bleak world. There are touching hints of virtue and dignity, creeping in almost unnoticed because they are so perfectly probable. There is Flora Finching's unobtrusive and self-sacrificing care for her "hair legacy," Mr. F.'s aunt. There is Mrs. Plornish's care for her father. There is even, in Chapter 29, a momentary softening, surprising, but not in the context unconvincing, of the perennial harshness of Mrs. Clennam, which leads her to kiss Amy with gentleness.

It is, certainly, a sad world where such virtues are needed at all. They are an inextricable mixture of truth and false-hood. As Dickens says of Little Dorrit's devotion to her father: "How true the light that shed false brightness round him." The same idea recurs when Clennam in his eagerness to help Doyce with his invention brings financial ruin upon him. It is a world where love does not find its proper object, where affections are misplaced, where kind-ness is muddled, but where the primary human affections unmistakably retain their primacy. To underline the point, the cynicism of Gowan is bitterly satirised.

At the same time Dickens's social indignation has softened into a benevolent scepticism about reforms and improve-ments, and his satire is more purely moral in its direction than ever before. He has become tender towards those, like Dorrit himself and Flora, who suffer from incurable illusions. He reserves his indignation for those who insulate themselves from all feeling. Perhaps the strength of his own emotions prevented him from taking the final step of pitying these also. But, as we have said before, he was not Dostoevsky. The religious dimension, which would have given coherence and deeper meaning to the withered and touching scraps of virtue displayed by Flora and Mrs. Plornish, and even by Mrs. Clennam—a triumph of fairness—this is absent. Even without it, *Little Dorrit* seems to be a very great novel. And those battered pieces of virtue are like palpably authentic archæological finds—half-understood fragments of a lost civilisation.

12

Great Expectations

Like *Hard Times*, *Great Expectations* suffers a little from over-correction of the characteristic failings of the early Dickens. He was determined to create a coherent unity at last; and perhaps a bit concerned also to prove to his critics that he could do so. It was natural for him to conceive unity partly in terms of harmonising images, and partly in terms of a neat plot. In the first he succeeded; the marshes, the hulks, the wedding-cake and many other images coalesce into an impression of decay and deceit and uncertainty, as subtle and satisfying as any the English novel can show. But a neat plot, in the hands of Dickens, even a mature Dickens, will never be quite free from melodrama. So we have a curious contrast at times between the book's tone, reminiscent, psychologically inquiring, morally penetrating, and some of its events which seem to belong to the world of the thriller. The whole conception of Orlick, for instance, seems out of keeping, and particularly the scene in which he lures Pip into an obvious trap, and allows a rescue, as so many murderers have done in detective stories since, by his endless explanations.[1]

[1] A valuable article by Julian Moynahan (*Essays in Criticism*, January, 1960) suggests that there is a transference of Pip's guilt on to Orlick, and that his function in the novel is psychologically important. Mr. Moynahan makes out a good case, but if it is accepted it would not invalidate the point made in the text.

Similarly, the fact that Pip's wealth comes from the convict, and its consequent connection with crime and brutality, is too obviously stressed in Chapter 32, when Wemmick takes Pip to see the prison, and the criminals among whom Jaggers works, and: " I consumed the whole time in thinking how strange it was that I should be encompassed by all this taint of prison and crime; that in my childhood out on our lonely marshes I should have first encountered it; that it should have reappeared on two occasions, starting out like a stain that was faded but not gone. . . ." The trouble here, of course, is the familiar one of the point of view. The narrator, who at this time has no idea that the convict will return and reveal himself as the founder of Pip's fortunes, cannot credibly be made to think all that the author wants said.

The unlikely bones of the story show through too, when Estella turns out exactly as Miss Havisham intended, and then blames her patron for her own lack of feeling. Estella speaks here rather in the style of a lawyer putting a case against Miss Havisham. But it is scarcely credible that she should bitterly lament the absence of feelings she has never had. In any case, would not this gloomy and solitary upbringing rather tend to encourage dreaming, a willingness to love, and even romantic illusions?

But there is another and more important sense in which the book represents a conscious correction of the author's past. Edgar Johnson says that *Great Expectations* is Dickens's penance for subservience to false values; and though the question may be more complicated than he allows, there is clearly a good deal of truth in this. When we recall Dickens's earlier assaults on rank and wealth, we are struck both by the subtlety and by the ambiguity of the satirical light cast upon them here. It is remarkable that no one in *Great Expectations* is free from the taint of servility towards rank and wealth.

Even in *Little Dorrit* Clennam is clear-sighted. But here everybody, including the kindhearted Herbert sees wealth through a romantic haze; even honest Joe's humble acceptance of Pip's sudden rise contains an unhealthy element of confusion between worth and fortune: " Which," he says, "you have that growed and that swelled, and that gentlefolked, as, to be sure, you are a honour to your king and country." At the same time, Magwitch, in his reckless generosity, curiously combines the almost accidental possession of great wealth with a servile admiration of the "gentlemanly" qualities he imagines it can bring to others.

All this suggests that we have here something a little different from a penance. For this protean admiration of wealth does not appear as an error to be repudiated, but as a universal and unexplained blight affecting good and bad men in different ways. The technique of story-telling, too, is better suited to the posing of ambiguous moral problems than to providing clear solutions to them. Pip tells his own story, and combines and at times confuses in a single narrative what he felt at the time, what he ought to have felt, and what later reflection made him feel. It is as if the author wished a little ambiguity to remain.

Why should this be? In part it fits well enough into the pattern of the author's mature development. He had become more aware of the mixture of human motives, of the unexpectedness of consequences. But Dickens was still capable of wielding sharp satirical blades; we look for another explanation of the faintness of moral condemnation, and we notice that Pip is almost alone among Dickens's characters in showing how things may appear in the eyes of the rich. Pip is, for instance, worried and bullied by his servant. He is irritable, bored and neurotic. His discontent excites sympathy even when he is being most contemptuous of others. There may be many reasons for this, but one is so very obvious that we may be inclined to overlook it altogether. Dickens was, after all, a very rich man in 1860, and he had no intention of ever being anything else. What may be called the mythical side of the story—the side that suggests by means of Magwitch that the wealth of society comes from tainted sources—is beautifully lucid. The past in which Pip's changing motives are weighed and judged is subtle and fascinating, but also elusive and ultimately inconclusive. In the person of Pip, Dickens was indeed striking at himself, as Edgar Johnson says, but he took good care not to strike too hard. He provided Pip (and himself) with many excuses, and allowed him to shelter behind the amiable failings of such fine fellows as Herbert and Joe Gargery.

In view of the deadly seriousness of the theme, it is hard not to feel, that at times things are a bit too jolly. Wemmick's castle and aged parent, schematically, seem to represent the divorce between business and private life, the tendency of the cash nexus to drive anyone possessing strong human sympathies into a futile longing for an imaginary past. There is a mournful, even tragic, pre-Raphaelite latent in the conception of Wemmick's character. But this interesting figure is never released. Wemmick's story is actually treated more in the style of *Nicholas Nickleby*. The innocent arm creeping round the waist of his beloved, his " Here's a church, let's get married" are amusing, but they really belong to a phase of Dickens's development that he could no longer recapture with full conviction. They belong to a past period when the laws of time and space and the limitations of human nature seemed like putty in the hands of a young genius of abounding energy and huge popularity.

But the main symbolical framework, which came into being at a deeper level of the mind than Wemmick's castle, is splendidly pervasive and never too obtrusive. The two leading ideas would seem to be parasitism and rejection from society. Living on unearned income is, of course, seen as parasitism; and it is reflected in a series of controlled echoes and parallels. Miss Havisham, after her disappointment, has developed into a kind of emotional *voyeur*, feeding upon the passions and illusions of the young, because they alone can persuade her that she is still capable of feeling—in its negative forms of revenge, deceit and frustration. Her enjoyment of Pip's mistake about the source of his money is essentially parasitic. She is not even capable now of active deceit. Pumblechook and the local tailor, bowing down before Pip's new greatness are going through the motions of a parasitism that cannot even feed. For Pip is himself a parasite, and will, in any case, give them nothing. Pip's social success is likewise unreal; he does not even achieve full acceptance as one of the " Finches of the Grove." And the Finches themselves are only copying without purpose the external formulas of Parliamentary procedure. Into this pattern details fit with beautiful naturalness. A very minor character, Jack at the Ship, has his interest in the recovery of Compeyson's body from the river "much heightened when he heard it had stockings on. Probably it took about a dozen drowned men to fit him out completely; and that may have been the reason why the different articles of his dress are in various stages of decay." Decay—parasitism and decay inevitably go together, and decay is at the centre of the symbolic structure, corresponding to the parasitic moral situation just outlined. Rot is by nature slow, pervasive and undramatic. It needs to be presented in many different guises to take full imaginative effect. The marsh, the rotting hulks, the Thames waterside, the wedding cake—none of them seems otiose or repetitive.

II

To carry the idea of exclusion from society there are two contrasted figures, Magwitch and Miss Havisham. One is the apparent and the other the real source of Pip's fortune; one is the guardian and the other the real father of the girl he loves. One is, in Pip's eyes, a delicate, awe-inspiring high-class female, the other is a despised ruffian, who admires Pip and is despised by him. But these contrasts serve also to draw our attention to deep similarities. Each lives outside normal society. Miss Havisham has rejected society, and entered a voluntary imprisonment. Magwitch is excluded from society by crime, by legal imprisonment, and then by transportation. The difficulty of returning to society, for Miss Havisham, is psychological; and the stubbornness of this barrier of feeling is suggested by the fact that when at last she begins to show normal feelings she undergoes an ordeal by fire, and narrowly escapes death. Magwitch can only return to society at the risk of incurring a sentence of death. All this is meant to show that the voluntary and the involuntary prisoner are bound by fetters of equal strength. To drive this home there is the melodramatic dual link with Compeyson.

The value of all this begins to become clear when we see how oblivious Pip is to the likeness. The grotesque paraphernalia of the Havisham mansion does not repel or alarm him. He feels that Miss Havisham, being rich or upper class (the two ideas are hardly separate in his mind), has a right to her eccentricities. So the shock of Magwitch's revelation does not merely consist in learning that there is a social gulf between himself and the Havisham-Estella household; the trouble is that Magwitch's theory of wealth is only a slightly cruder version of Pip's own. Pip has worshipped Miss Havisham's insolent use of wealth; and now the despised convict is asking him to use it with a similar insolence. And Magwitch wants him to do what he has always intended to do, to live as a fine gentleman on someone else's money. So Pip is forced to realise that his horror of Magwitch is irrational; and hence to question everything he had taken for granted. But nothing positive replaces the shattered dream; and his renunciation is deeply ironical. For he renounces his wealth and position, with much conscious nobility, but he does so on snobbish principles. For Magwitch's Australian fortune has been fairly earned. The inadequacy of his change of heart is conveyed with fine symbolic appropriateness when pathetically he tries to repay his debt to Magwitch, not yet knowing him to be the cause of all his wealth: " He [the messenger] came faithfully, and he brought me the two one-pound notes. I was a poor boy then, as you know, and to a poor boy they were a little fortune. But like you, I have done well since, and you must let me pay them back. You can put them to some other poor boy's use." Pip can be seen as the image of the philanthropy of the rich, not really giving, but repaying a tiny part of what they have received.

Suggested parallels of this kind throughout the book are at once indefinite and pervasive. More than anything else they prevent the image of parasitism from becoming a merely limiting factor. From the brief analysis of this image offered above, it might be supposed that the book was only about a sort of respectable underworld of shady and greedy money-worshippers. But the book as a whole, on the contrary, gives an irresistible impression of portraying society as a whole. *Great Expectations* is not, like *David Copperfield* and like so many English and French novels of the nineteenth century, the story of a young man growing up and gradually shedding illusions and being assimilated to society's ways. Society fawns on him. Pumblechook recognises his superiority. Even Joe shares some of his illusions. There seems to be a conspiracy to treat money as an independent self-created entity, worthy of reverence. Hardly anyone in the book works productively. Magwitch's fortune was made by work, certainly; but far away, by methods unknown to the reader. So the solitary exception that counts is Joe Gargery. His forge is the only reminder of the necessity of work, of the connection between skill and wealth. In a book full of soft, hazy images, of mists and marshes, and full also of hazy mental processes, Joe's forge is a hard fact, represented by iron and fire.

Pip's erratic fortunes begin and end with Joe, who gives up the advantage of having Pip as an apprentice, and finally pays off the debts which are all that remain of Pip's wealth and expectations. The forge is indeed a moving image of the dignity of work. But Joe, too, as we have seen is in his innocent, unselfish way a snob. Even Joe is on the fringe of the conspiracy to regard money as sacred.

It is at this point, it seems to me, that we reach a fascinating and intractable dilemma of criticism. Are we to say that Dickens in the end faltered before the devastating satirical demands that the book's plan should have imposed? The symbolic suggestiveness of Pip's position in society (for instance, the meaning of his utterly inadequate offer or repayment to Magwitch, mentioned above) is unwontedly vague. And the vagueness is reflected in another uncertainty of a technical character. From what point of view is the story told? Ostensibly it comes from the mature, disillusioned Pip. But this is hardly satisfactory. The neat, comfortable and moderately lucrative business position, which is Pip's haven when the storms of expectation are over, is scarcely a suitable place from which to adjudicate on a capitalist society's attitude to money and class. And Pip's own final attitude is never clear. Does he reject all unearned wealth? Does he come to realise his own inconsistency about the excellence of accepting money from Miss Havisham and the degradation of accepting it from Magwitch? Pip can indeed comprehend his past mistakes, but he cannot in retrospect effectively judge the society in which he had lived.

This line of argument, which tends to show that the book, for all its brilliance, in the end stifles unworthily the moral problems it raises, might receive powerful support from the ending. The fact that the "unhappy ending" was altered at an outsider's request is perhaps not very important. I agree, myself, with those who regard the "happy" ending actually published as representing best the author's intentions and the book's own logic. It is fitting that Pip should frustrate Miss Havisham's designs on Estella just as he has frustrated Magwitch's plans to make him rich. But it is still a most ambiguous ending. What is Pip really getting in the person of Estella? Mr. Hillis Miller makes this interesting comment: " Pip now has all that he wanted, Estella and her jewels, but what he has is altogether different from what he expected. Rather than possessing the impossible reconciliation of freedom and security he had sought in Estella and gentility, he now loves and is loved by another fallible and imperfect human being like himself." This would seem to be good summary of what Dickens intended. But Mr. Miller makes no allowance for the artistic failure which must surely be involved if this interpretation is right. For how are we to believe that Estella has changed enough to be worth having?

The book ends with a characteristically ambiguous amalgam of mist and light. " I took her hand in mine, and we went out of the ruined place; and, as the morning mists had risen long ago when I first left the forge, so, the evening mists were rising now, and in all the broad expanse of tranquil light they showed to me, I saw no shadow of another parting from her." It is an ending which leaves many questions open. It does not rule out the possibility that Pip has yet another terrible disillusionment in store. Is this ambiguity also a sign of a new timidity in Dickens, and of a faltering grasp?

Such a line of criticism may seem strong or weak to different people. But it is, in any case, not conclusive. It could be argued that all this vagueness and ambiguity is perfectly appropriate; moreover, that it is implicit in the book's whole plan, as the persistent images of mist and marsh, the persistent weariness and decay clearly show. It would then follow that Dickens was not here timid or muddled. Practised craftsman that he had now become, he merely understood the necessary limits of satire. Satire can attack the vices of society, but it cannot effectively attack society itself. If it makes the attempt, it must degenerate into a mere tirade, a fictionalised pamphlet. (A study of some of Zola's failures would be instructive here.) Dickens, the argument would run, was now humble enough to realise that he, too, was a man and a member of society; that there was no easy solution to the moral problems raised by money; that even palpable injustices could seldom be fairly blamed on any individual. Moreover, in this way, the theme of alienation from society could acquire an additional force. According to the book's own logic the satirist who rejects and condemns society utterly is not the brave and shining rebel he is so often represented as being. He is, ultimately, of the same party as Magwitch and Miss Havisham. His intentions may be excellent; but he is a dying limb cut from the body. On this view, then, Dickens went as far as was reasonably possible in exposing the unreality of dreams of wealth, but he wisely showed the question complete with all the mysterious ambiguity it actually assumes in life.

Personally, I cannot see that either of these lines of argument has the power to refute the other. The study of this great novel ends with a question mark.

I3

Our Mutual Friend

The first two chapters of *Our Mutual Friend* make a perfect contrast. The third shows an unexpected connection between two opposite worlds. In this technical arrangement Dickens presented in its simplest form a dominating idea of a novel that would attain great complexity. The essential contrast is between depth and surface. We begin with the unforgettable picture of Gaffer Hexam's boat drifting on the tide—the picture of the bird of prey, the scavenger who feeds on the possessions of the dead. His livelihood emerges from the unknown depths of the river, just as, speaking figuratively, it comes from an untraced underworld of crime and misery and anonymity. The third paragraph gives the keynote:

> Allied to the bottom of the river rather than to its surface, by reason of the slime and ooze with which it was covered, and its sodden state, this boat and the two figures in it obviously were doing something that they often did, and were seeking what they often sought.

Hexam is of the depths not simply because of his moral depravity, and the secrecy of his way of life, but in another sense also, as we realise when we come to Chapter 2, which describes the Veneerings' dinner. The name Veneering gives a hint which is scarcely needed. This is a superficial world, where old friendship means that people met yesterday, where love and hate are alike feigned (cf. Lady Tippins's list of lovers, odious men and traitors), where every emotion can be expressed except the only one that can really be felt—boredom.

Unless we keep this fundamental contrast between depth and surface clearly before us, we shall be unable to do justice to the very specialised type of success achieved in the presentation of the Veneerings and their circle. The nearest parallel in Dickens's own work is the Circumlocution Office in *Little Dorrit*. The treatment cannot properly be called satirical. For there is little sense of Veneerings and Podsnaps as human beings, with real responsibilities, joys and sorrows. Instead, we have a highly stylised portrait of the superficial aspects of a certain kind of commercial and social success. The only people present at the Veneerings' dinner-table who are presented as human are Wrayburn and Lightwood, who provide the link between the immeasurably distant worlds of the first two chapters. But their humanity, too, is in abeyance while they dine at the Veneerings'. They, too, go through the movements of the customary solemn and fatuous dance. They are all being watched from a position from which humanity is invisible. They are accurate silhouettes, without a millimetre of depth.

Thus, in the second chapter, Mortimer Lightwood, shown in different company to be a man of warm feelings, and a certain indolent sense of responsibility, begins to tell the story of John Harmon, the Boffin inheritance, and the husband chosen for Bella Wilfer. And he tells it thus:

He chose a husband for her, entirely to his own satisfaction and not in the least to hers, and proceeded to settle upon her, as her marriage portion, I don't know how much Dust, but something immense. At this stage of the affair the poor girl respectfully intimated that she was secretly engaged to that popular character whom the novelists and versifiers call Another, and that such a marriage would make Dust of her heart and Dust of her life—in short, would set her up, on a very extensive scale, in her father's business.

He tells the story, in fact, as a stock comic melodrama; it is not that he really lacks sympathy; he is simply playing the Veneering game in the approved fashion. It is hardly possible, in their presence, to play any other. So, in view of the pervasive contrast of this world with the physical and moral depths of the river, it is fair to say that the treatment of the Veneerings and Podsnaps is not superficial. It is a serious and sensitive account of the superficial aspect of things. And it affects our sense of the meaning of the river's depth. Because it is contrasted with something superficial and bad, the river's depth has two opposite meanings waiting to be used. It can be degradation, but it can also be profundity. The degradation comes first, but, as we shall see, Dickens carefully hoarded the potentialities of the other meaning.

The two worlds, infinitely remote in thought, are physically close. Each is really involved with the other. That is why Lightwood and Wrayburn are called from the unmeaning dinner-party to the mystery of the unknown dead body, and Eugene says of it: "Not much worse than Lady Tippins." The grotesque comment is quite in character, and it makes the connection with an economy, which Dickens took many years to learn. Like the Inspector of Police, who inquires into the causes of this death, Wrayburn and Lightwood are, in their absurd way, concerned with the practice of law. The inspector is named the Abbott of the Monastery, to show his detachment from the real life of the river. All three illustrate the remoteness of official England from the underworld of the river.

II

Our Mutual Friend has its weakly melodramatic side. But in the main, its tortuous plot is thoroughly serious. It reveals unexpected but real links between people and classes that suspect no connection at all. The characteristic humorous-grotesque (" Not much worse than Lady Tippins") could have occurred at any time in Dickens's career. But its connection with a large-scale plan of comparison of opposites was possible to the mature Dickens only. Similar "impossible" connections are established when Wrayburn marries Lizzie Hexam, and when the schoolmaster Headstone, becomes involved with Riderhood. The strength of the bonds is revealed, perhaps too obviously, when these two plunge into the river and die together in an indissoluble embrace of hatred.

As an image of the cumbersome structure of society, the idea of depth and surface was natural and simple, representing dregs and cream—the polite world on top, the seething, half-known world of misery and crime below. But in another way, it was paradoxical and surprising. For the implication was that the sophisticated few were simple, stupid and easy to understand, while the unlettered many were complex and intractable. There was a touch of topsy-turvy here. It was entirely deliberate; and it was to be developed into one of the book's dominating ideas. There is the scene where charity becomes an avenging demon pursuing Betty Higden. There is the extraordinary reversed parent and child relationship of Jenny Wren and her father. And there is the case of the money-lending partnership of Fledgeby and Riah. Riah, drawn in the image of the stock literary character of the grasping Jew is really as near to sanctity as Dickens's imagination could reach. Fledgeby, with his air of lazy aristocratic boredom, is the grasping man of business. This last case, of course, is merely a reversal of a literary cliché, while the first two examples are monstrous reversals of the normal order of things. But all such instances are generalised into a symbolic physical form in a remarkable chapter (Pt. II Chap. 5) where the peace of the high roof-garden where Riah and Jenny Wren sit is compared to the grave, and where Jenny calls to the frightened Fledgeby, " Come back and be dead."

All this amounts to far more than a rhetorical device. It was an outward sign of a new flexibility in Dickens. He had never at any time been reluctant to imagine violence and cruelty. But the cruelty of, say, Dotheboys Hall, however painful, had been predictable. It was the cruelty of the strong towards the weak. But here there is a new type of cruelty (even sadism) in the imagination of the weak and innocent Jenny Wren:

" If you were treated as you ought to be," she says to her drunken father, " you'd be fed upon the skewers of cats' meat; only the skewers after the cats had had the meat." And she goes on to picture what she would if " He " (her dream husband) should prove to be a drunkard: " I'd make a spoon red hot, and I'd have some boiling liquor bubbling in a saucepan, and I'd take it out hissing, and I'd open his mouth with the other hand—or perhaps he'd sleep with his mouth ready open—and I'd pour it down his throat, and blister it and choke him." Who were really the weak and who the strong? Who were the oppressors? It had once seemed so easy to say, and now the answer was always ambiguous. Perhaps no one was more suited than Dickens to the making of such ambiguities. For as moral problems came to seem more doubtful and difficult, the paradisal clearness and intensity of Dickens's pictorial imagination remained in all its purity. Even when pursuing moral ambiguities, he was incapable of leaving a blurred impression.

Another strange relationship is that of Wrayburn and Headstone. The pursuer is the tormented one, and the pursued is the tormentor. Even when Headstone finally makes a murderous attack on Wrayburn, it is still the latter who remains coolly in control of the situation, and his sufferings afterwards are as nothing compared with Headstone's.

III

Dickens was already an experienced symbolist before he wrote *Our Mutual Friend*; but in the leading symbols here, the river and the dust-heap, he was able, perhaps for the first time, to unite two opposite strands of his personality and art. Here Dickens the fantastic, melodramatic symbolist, and Dickens the hypnotic recorder of the dingy detail of life, were at last reconciled.

In the course of the book many of the leading characters fall into the river. Either they are drowned, or they emerge new men. John Harmon emerges with a new name and a new personality. Eugene Wrayburn's narrow escape from drowning after the murderous attack on him by Headstone marks the time when he has at last overcome the view natural to a man of his class and indolent habits that Lizzie can only be his prey. When he falls in, it is, of course, Lizzie who pulls him out, just as her influence has saved him from weariness and cynicism. So far, we have an obvious and (some people may feel) a rather prissy and unreal little allegory. But Dickens no longer presents things only in such simple colours. For it is the training she received from her

father that enables Lizzie to save Wrayburn's life. The
source of pure love is the parasite who preys upon the dead.
And the river is the corrupted provider of his livelihood.
The river is death to Headstone and Riderhood. It is the
source, or at least a visible sign of new life for Harmon and
Wrayburn. It is hard to resist the idea that the river has a
sacramental, baptismal character. It is a mystery bringing
salvation or damnation as it is received worthily or unworthily.

When we read some of the descriptions Dickens gives us
of the river, there is no burking the fact that this is a
grotesque idea. " The wheels rolled on, and rolled down by
the Monument, and by the Tower, and by the Docks; down
by Ratcliffe, and by Rotherhithe; down by where accumulated scum of humanity seemed to be washed from higher
grounds, like so much moral sewage, and to be pausing until
its own weight forced it over the bank and sunk it in the
river." Strange if this is equated with the pure waters of
baptism. And we may well feel doubtful too, because of
Dickens's own religious outlook. The sacramental, and (in
the theological sense) mysterious was alien to his simple,
benevolent pietistic protestantism.

I am not trying to invent an Anglo-Catholic Dickens, and,
if I were, no one would believe in him. But to be impressed
imaginatively by the symbolism associated with sacramental
doctrines is an entirely different thing from accepting the
doctrines themselves.[1] And the fact is that, whatever
objections we may feel, the interpretation I am somewhat
hesitantly offering is in the text. Here are Lizzie's thoughts
when her father's dead body is dragged from the river and
placed upon the shore: " Father, was that you calling me?
Was it you, the voiceless and the dead? Was it you, thus

[1] For a detailed discussion of this vital distinction between symbol and
sacrament in the case of another great Protestant symbolist, Spenser, the
reader is referred to Professor C. S. Lewis's ' *The Allegory of Love* '.

buffeted as you lie here in a heap? Was it you, thus *baptized unto Death*, with these flying impurities now flung upon your face?" And on reflection, we come to see, I think, that the grotesqueness of the filthy Thames as a baptismal stream is very Dickensian. It combines his love of the high, inclusive symbol, his obsession with dirt and squalor, and his deep interest in the physical detail of the London of his time. Opposite as they are in many ways, Dickens and Flaubert had this in common—they naturalised, vulgarised, if you like, the poetic symbol. In this, surely, they were true novelists, for the novel is the most realistic of literary forms. The old poetic symbol, still used in the novel by Dickens's contemporaries and successors, by Hawthorne and sometimes by Henry James, may seem, when compared with the "natural" symbols of Dickens, an interloper from an alien form of art. In the way he superimposed the low, criminal figures of Hexam and Riderhood upon the seething symbolism of the river, Dickens showed the tact of a great artist. There was bound to be a resistance in his readers to the transformation of a familiar sight of London into an image of the mystery of life and death. Hexam and Riderhood are adapted to soothe doubts about high-flown idealism. And in the light of the redemptive action of the river upon Harmon and Wrayburn, the odd, neutral scene where Riderhood just escapes drowning becomes unexpectedly significant:

Doctor examines the dank carcase, and pronounces, not hopefully, that it is worth while trying to reanimate the same. . . . No one has the least regard for the man: with them all, he has been an object of avoidance, suspicion, and aversion; but the spark of life within him is curiously separable from himself now, and they have a deep interest in it, probably because it *is* life, and they are living and must die.

This is the bedrock minimum of human dignity. This is a man to whom the river means nothing but a criminal livelihood; and to whom the baptismal mystery means nothing at all. His daughter catches a momentary glimpse of it; she has a "vague idea that the old evil is drowned out of him," but "The short-lived delusion begins to fade. The low, bad, unimpressible face is coming up from the depths of the river, or what other depths, to the surface again." And when he recovers his wits, Riderhood angrily asserts that nothing has really happened, and that the concern felt for him by others is useless interference.

This short scene achieves three important things at once. It provides a necessary contrast to the "spiritual" nature of the immersion of Hexam and Wrayburn. That is, it recalls our attention to the dull impassivity of average human nature—its overwhelming tendency to reject, despise or ignore appeals to its moral sensibilities, its wish to forget that the knowledge of good and evil is possible to men.

Similarly, the scene helps to prevent the regenerative power of the river in other cases from seeming too like a facile convenience. It reminds us that a gift can be refused. Finally, Riderhood's escape ironically prepares the way for the moment when he is drowned, locked in Headstone's grasp. The waterside superstition, which makes him say, " I have been brought out o' drowning, and I can't be drowned," has a parallel perhaps accidentally close in theology. Riderhood is in the position of a man who "can afford to sin" because he has once received grace. His drowning is the proper nemesis for such an attitude. It is a nice point, too, that it is Riderhood, who has rejected the experience the river offers, who is the lock-keeper, placed in charge of the river's traffic by the powers that be. The criminal scavenger is also the official; and this reinforces the idea suggested by Betty Higden's death, where official charity plays a murderer's part. And in her despair, she hears the river whispering, "Come to me, come to me! When the cruel shame and terror you have so long fled from, most beset you, come to me! I am the Relieving Officer appointed by eternal ordinance to do my work; I am not held in estimation according as I shirk it. My breast is softer than the pauper-nurse's; death in my arms is peacefuller than among the pauper wards. Come to me!" The river can mean both life and death. But in either role it is at odds with a lifeless official routine, which has neither vitality nor the momentous dignity of death.

IV

I am not inclined to deny that the symbolism of the river is a little tedious towards the end. Perhaps it is too neat when the Wilfer-Rokesmith wedding breakfast is held in a room overlooking the river, and when Bella and Lizzie walk by the riverbank when Bella is about to reach a great decision. But minor extravagances cannot impair the grandeur and flexibility or the unusual visual reality of this great symbolic conception. This phrase might also fit the other dominating symbol, the dust heap. It has been shown that the story of the dust heaps is less fantastic than it is likely to appear to us. They were the source of great fortunes in early Victorian times, they frequently did contain buried treasures such as Wegg hoped to find, and (as an attentive reader would be inclined to guess) they were largely composed of human dung.[1] As in most of Dickens's fantasies, there is an indisputable basis of fact. The heaps are first mentioned in Mortimer Lightwood's strange narrative to the Veneerings, which gives the first details of John Harmon's story: " He

---

[1] See Humphry House: *The Dickens World* for an excellent discussion of the economic background here. Mayhew, however, gives a much more varied composition for the dust heaps.

[Harmon's father] grew rich as a Dust Contractor, and lived in a hollow in a hilly country entirely composed of Dust. On his own small estate the growling old vagabond threw up his own mountain range, like an old volcano, and its geological formation was dust."

This passage introduces an atmosphere of fairytale which never ceases to cling to the occupation and personality of the Golden Dustman, Boffin who inherits the mounds. His title, Golden Dustman, so often repeated, belongs to fairytale, but like many fairytales, it is notably susceptible of Freudian interpretation, a type of interpretation which Dickens might not have found altogether startling. Certainly the money-dirt connection was already present to his mind. By now we have no need to be surprised either at being asked to have one foot in fairyland and one in the grimy realities of Victorian commerce.

The symbolic meaning of the mounds is shaped with unobtrusive skill. The studied refusal to face the eeriness of money visible in this form, and the cheerful normality of Boffin (during the first half of the book) contribute to it. " I may sell them, though I should be sorry to see the neighbourhood deprived of 'em too. It'll look but a poor dead flat without the Mounds." We are almost tricked into thinking that this is as normal as having money in the bank. But then the last chapter of Book I ("A Dismal Swamp") introduces a new idea. Here the mounds are imaginatively linked with the primeval slime—an idea at this date already alive with haunting evolutionary echoes, as we can see from *In Memoriam*. The primeval slime becomes an equivalent of the commercial underworld from which a great Victorian fortune might emerge.

But there is another way in which the mounds truly represent the character of Boffin's fortune. They are uselessly fixed there. And *Our Mutual Friend* is, in part, a story of the ineffectiveness of money. Boffin can neither use money for his own benefit, nor for the benefit of others. Entrance into polite society is an obvious chimera for a man of his stamp. Generosity and friendliness are wasted on men like Wegg and Venus. Good causes may take on the aspect of the Avenging Angel, which Betty Higden saw, or become only a series of elegant and meaningless committees.

Boffin's transformation into a miser is puzzling. It has been plausibly suggested that his final confession that he was deliberately acting a miser's part was an afterthought of Dickens. It hardly matters whether this is so or not; in any case, the confession is totally unconvincing. There can be no doubt that in the miserly passages, especially as Boffin listens to the grotesque stories of misers past, a very deep excitement spreads into the writing. Though it cannot be demonstrated, it seems to me, that this excitement is, in a special way, personal to the author, in excess of the literary requirements of the story. We may tentatively conclude that these passages represent an attempt to work out a personal dilemma. There is abundant evidence that Dickens was the victim of a set of incompatible obsessions about money. These are especially obvious whenever money is linked with dirt, as it is here, not only because of the mounds, but by the tales from the book about misers, which are all physically unclean and squalid (e.g. the story of the mutton pies). We should notice, too, that in a crazy way, Boffin is being logical when he begins to adopt a miser's outlook. He has been thwarted in every attempt to achieve anything with his money. Unless he abandons his interest in it altogether, he can only turn to money itself as end instead of means.

Dickens himself was no miser. But there is a reflection here of a restless and dissatisfied spirit. And the extreme literary ineptitude of the handling of Boffin's recantation, perpetrated in the full maturity of his huge artistic powers, must surely indicate a moral inconsistency. It was in his nature to despise money, to earn it in vast sums, to adore it, to spend it with pointless extravagance. A consistent moral or economic view of it was beyond him. Nevertheless, it is doubtful whether the fascination of money has ever been better conveyed than in *Our Mutual Friend*.

Boffin's recantation is not the only thing amiss with the closing chapters. The Wilfer story takes a plunge into sentimentality. The beating up of Fledgeby is an unconvincing and nasty episode. This study has throughout stressed Dickens's amazing powers of development. So we must not evade the decline which occurs towards the end of one of his finest books—the last he was to complete. Two reasons for it stand out—his ambivalent attitude to money, and another which is creditable to him. As we have seen the contrast between depth and surface is fundamental to the book. Dickens valiantly tried to provide a final reconciliation between the classes, an end to perennial conflicts. This is the meaning of the marriage of Wrayburn and Lizzie Hexam. But this majestic reconciliation of implacable forces was beyond him. He was not Dante; he had a towering imagination, capable of presenting opposing forces with unequalled power. But he had no peace within, from which to endow his imagined world with peace. For this reason there is always something a little depressing about the happy endings invented by this tortured spirit.

14

Conclusion

At the start the questions were posed, " How did a man with such a coarse mind become a master of his art? " and " How was it possible, in the nineteenth century to be a classic and a best-seller at the same time? " For, of course, the nineteenth century was the first in which a vast half-educated reading public appeared to disturb the cultivated standards of the much smaller class of readers in earlier times. Part of the answer will now, I hope, be clear. We have seen how dully literal Dickens could be over such a question as the medical accuracy of Spontaneous Combustion, as described in *Bleak House*. And we have seen sufficient examples of his obsessive devotion to detail. Both these are obvious lowbrow traits. But they could also become, in the special circumstances of Dickens's work, major artistic assets. For the novel is the most concrete of all literary forms. It can never afford to ignore the questions, how, when and where? The novelist must make his spade a spade before it can ever be a symbol. This is a general truth, but it has a particularly strong application to a novelist whose subject is the swarming urban life of the nineteenth century, and a new civilisation deeply modified by the machine.

Dickens throughout his life showed little spiritual development, and only a limited degree of intellectual development. It is in his symbolism that we can most easily see the kind of development he did achieve. Many symbolic novelists have an idea, and then think of an image that will carry it. Dickens hardly ever did this. His symbols were presented to him by the natural constitution of his mind and by his early experience. When he came of age in 1833, he was already obsessed with prisons, with crowds, with the mystery of money, with squalor, dirt and violence. The story of his development is partly that he penetrated deeper and deeper into the treasures of meaning that they contained. As he probed into their multiple implications, they became symbols of their own accord.

Here again, he had an advantage as a lowbrow, for it is very commonplace ideas like these that are inexhaustible. If his obsessions had been less ordinary, his imaginative development might not have been so formidably complete.

We have seen, for instance, in *Dombey and Son*, what he could do with a literary cliché. He took the stock poetic ideas of the river of time and the sea of eternity, and turned them into symbols packed with contemporary meanings. Take, for instance, these lines of Matthew Arnold, who was some years his junior:

> An air of coolness plays upon his face,
> And an unwonted calm pervades his breast.
> And then he thinks he knows
> The hills where his life rose,
> And the sea where it goes.
>
> (*The Buried Life*)

This has its own beauty; but it would clearly be impossible to link it effectively with Brighton, with fashionable schools, and a doctor urging an exhausted woman to make an effort. Dickens easily, thoughtlessly almost, achieved the impossible leap, and turned a poetic symbol, already venerable and a trifle weary, into a novelist's symbol, full of exciting possibilities. A certain coarseness, an insensitivity to finer feelings were necessary for this task. Here Dickens the lowbrow ignoramus, the popular entertainer, merges into the person of the great artist.

Nearly all the most popular literary works of the nineteenth century were melodramas. *Murder in the Red Barn*, *Lady Audley's Secret*, Carlyle's *French Revolution* and Macaulay's history differ widely in quality, no doubt, but they were all very popular, and all intensely melodramatic. Now, as we have seen, one of Dickens's leading ideas, involved with some of his best, and some of his worst devices of plot, was that we are members one of another. Solemnly consecrated though this idea is by religious tradition, in literary terms it is very closely related to melodrama. Coincidences, long-lost sons, buried wills, hidden relationships—all these are crude statements of the idea that we are linked much more closely than we realise with people we have never seen. Vulgar in his tastes, and towering in imagination, Dickens seized eagerly upon the ridiculous paraphernalia of English melodrama. He enjoyed overobvious comparisons, like the wine running through the gutters and foreshadowing the blood bath of the Revolution in *A Tale of Two Cities*.

But the melodrama Dickens at first so carelessly copied was capable of enormous development, for its simple stock of ideas has very deep psychological roots. What could be more naïve and melodramatic, and at the same time more subtle and serious than the following passage from *Great Expectations*? The child Pip is watching the terrifying convict depart:

As I saw him go, picking his way among the nettles, and

among the brambles that bound the green mounds, he looked in my young eyes as if he were eluding the hands of dead people, stretching up cautiously out of their graves, to get a twist upon his ankle and pull him in.

We have all read articles about the influence of heredity on crime. But this idea, which we associate, perhaps rather wearily with "social science," here plunges down to a far deeper mental level, the level at which artistic appeals are made. And the means by which it reaches this point of depth is very near to the traditional macabre and childish melodrama. Dickens was at the same time a rather naïve conservative-liberal reformer, a lover of the fantastic, and an original artist fashioning new symbolic equivalents for our most inarticulate emotions. It is in this cluster of contradictions that much of the fascination of his work resides.

His slowness to grasp general ideas did not prove a handicap to the kind of achievements for which he was best fitted. Symbolic meanings seep slowly through the mass of accumulated detail, the wonderful topographical intimacy, the jostling contemporary problems. Gigantic failures like Melville's " Pierre " bear witness how ill-fitted the novel is to bear a condition where the idea triumphs and the fact is defeated. The ambiguities of Dickens's river in *Our Mutual Friend* or the slowly-developing meaning of the sea in *Dombey and Son* are only tolerable because they emerge hesitantly out of an undeniable physical reality.

So, in the end, his lack of intellectual consistency, already castigated in these pages, and the neurotic instability of the man's feelings, hardly matter, because the vivid journalist, the entertainer and the artist are triumphantly at one.

*Dates of the first publication in
serial or book form of the works
by Dickens discussed at length
in the text:*

Pickwick Papers (1836-37)
Oliver Twist (1837-39)
Nicholas Nickleby (1838-39)
The Old Curiosity Shop (1840-41)
Barnaby Rudge (1841)
Martin Chuzzlewit (1843-44)
Dombey and Son (1846-48)
David Copperfield (1849-50)
Bleak House (1852-53)
Hard Times (1854)
Little Dorrit (1855-57)
A Tale of Two Cities (1859)
Great Expectations (1860-61)
Our Mutual Friend (1864-65)
Edwin Drood (1870) unfinished

INDEX